all is ONE

Seth Falconer

For Annie and Dave

Published by Graysonian Press
www.graysonian.com
pat@graysonian.com
+27 11 4311274

Copyright © 2011 Seth Falconer

All rights reserved under international copyright conventions.
No part of this book may be reproduced, stored in a retrieval system, or transmitted in any form or by any means electronic, mechanical, photocopying, recorded or otherwise without written permission from Graysonian Press.

Whilst every care has been taken to check the accuracy of the information in this book, the publisher cannot be held responsible for any errors, omissions or originality.

Cover design www.timothymorrison.info

Photographs by Matt Kay – udontknowmattyk.wordpress.com

ISBN 978-0-9869902-0-5

Biography

Seth Falconer is a young South African who enjoys the company of chickens and growing his own food. Seth has sailed the width of the South Pacific Ocean and worked on a long-line fishing boat in New Zealand. He has practiced Reiki in between painting a house in South Africa's Eastern Cape and sculpting bronze furniture. He has taught English to four year olds in Taiwan and learned to enjoy Turkish tea. Seth has a deep passion for writing, the world of metaphysics, travelling and appreciating the simple things in life alongside his beautiful wife Claire.

Acknowledgements

By virtue of the truth that All is One, I cannot claim the credit for this work. It instead should be shared amongst us all, as it is from our collective will for spiritual growth that this book has come. However, due to the duality through which we live out our lives, I would like to give special thanks to a few people who have been particularly involved in my part of the writing of this book. To my parents: without your love and guidance I would never have been able to play the role I have in the realisation of All is One. A massive thanks to my beautiful wife Claire, for the countless hours of editing, love and support that she has selflessly given. Last but not least thank you to the team at Graysonian Press for transforming these words into the book it is today.

Introduction

It is only now, upon the imminent completion of this book, that I can clearly see the path along which this philosophy has led me. I find that with the gift of hindsight I can see where this section of my life's journey began, through an experience which I have up until now presumed to be totally separate from the writing of this book.

Of course, in truth, every instant of our lives is one of divine purpose and importance. The effects of the tiniest actions can, and do, change the course of our lives. With this in mind, I suppose I could begin this part of my story at any point in my past. My birth, on the eleventh of August 1984 would seem like a logical landmark, or maybe losing my first tooth, starting school or getting my first job. However, I now understand that although these were momentous moments in the life of Seth, they bear just as much sway over the rest of my life as any other moment in a long succession leading back in time.

Every instant exists within a complex web, the web of life whose tangled strands criss-cross the paths of our lives to create fantastic moments of synchronicity – moments that uncover the mysteries of the universe. Therefore, this book was probably born within the web of life long before I existed, perhaps in the lives and thoughts of my parents, or their parents, or their parents' parents, or in everything that occurred before them and everything that has occurred between then and now.

So it is with a certain degree of impossibility that I pinpoint the moment that All is One was born into my life. Perhaps I should say that I now see when the desire to write this book became tangibly visible to me. I can see what event sprouted the questions in my mind – the questions that led to the answers I have recorded within these pages.

All is One

It began in a sterile hotel room that could have been anywhere in the world, but happened to be in a small town in Taiwan. As a result of the lack of direction I had for some years prior to that night, my partner (later to become my wife) and I had left our comfortable lives in South Africa in search of something different. It was our second night in this strange and unfathomable land. We were lying wide awake late that night due to a combination of jetlag and the swarm of mosquitoes that buzzed around us. Our stomachs churned uneasily trying to digest a plateful of foreign food only just palatable to our Western mouths. In truth, the food and mosquitoes are receiving more credit for our wakefulness than they deserve. The chief culprit was really the knowledge that at nine the next morning, a short lady who spoke only a dozen words, understandable to our foreign ears, was going to arrive to pick us up for a teaching demonstration, something that neither of us had done before.

In an effort to distract myself from the feelings of nausea and fatigue that were running rife through my sleepless body, I began to tell Claire about a movie I had seen just before we left South Africa. The film was about how we, as people, are responsible for the creation of our own realities. This idea itself was something that we had both come across before but up until then had done little with. Out of desperation we decided to put the theory to the test.

The thought of our imminent demos was too unsettling at the time, so to distract ourselves, we decided to talk about what sort of a home we hoped to find. Taiwan, being one of the most densely-populated countries in the world, has no excess space and whatever is available is quickly snapped up and developed. We held little hope for anything bigger than a single room and if we were lucky, a bathroom with a decent-sized shower. However, more as a game than anything else, we began talking about the essence of the home we would like to find and after a while began to feel a little more confident. So, as was described in the film, we wrote out our 'requirements' in a positive affirmation-like format. It came out something like this:

We are so grateful for:
1. *A place with enough space for all of our various interests and hobbies.*
2. *A quiet place to meditate and do yoga.*
3. *A view with a fresh breeze and place to have a few plants.*
4. *Somewhere close to work for both of us.*

We then took turns reading our wishes out loud, each time focusing on feeling grateful for our beautiful home.

Eventually the next morning arrived and we miraculously managed to fumble our way through our demos, to the approval of our prospective employers. One thing led to another and before we knew it our new boss showed us the apartment that the school offered along with the job. Claire and I were dumbfounded as we walked into our new home. It had three bedrooms, one for us, one for friends and one for yoga and meditation. It had two bathrooms, one with a bath and one with a shower. It had a big open lounge and two balconies, both big enough to house numerous pot plants. When we opened the doors the mountain breeze flowed through the apartment. One balcony overlooked picturesque rice paddies, and the other our school. We lived literally next door. Even though the school had only been looking for one new English teacher, they offered us both full-time jobs, jobs that we stayed at happily for the duration of our time in the country.

Yes, one could always say that it was all one big coincidence, but as the person standing in that doorway, I knew with absolute certainty that it was not. How it happened I did not know, but I knew that we were there because of the 'gratitude' we had offered together the night before.

'How could that have happened?' was a question that travelled with me for a long time afterwards. I now see that it was this question that gave birth to this book. In the months and years that followed, ideas, inspiration and information came to me through numerous sources. Some came from people I had known for a long time and some from people I had just met. Some of it I saw in the events taking place around me, and some of it I read in books. Some of it simply seemed to appear in my head at the right time.

All is One is broken up into two different parts. The first part of the book is dedicated to understanding where humankind fits into the universal picture, where we come from and why. It explores humankind's inherently creative nature and how it is that we each create our own realities. In addition, Part One explores the collective ability of our creative nature and how humankind as a single entity creates a reality in which we all share.

Part Two highlights specific areas of our existence that need to be addressed if we are going to be able to restore balance to our world. It suggests ways in which we can use our creative nature to learn to control our future, and in so doing, begin creating a world where peace, love and harmony prevail.

It is important to bear in mind, especially as you read Part One, that this book was not designed to be read in a single sitting. Although it is somewhat shorter than many contemporary counterparts, it should take you just as long, if not longer, to read. The manner in which it has been written necessitates that it be read within a quiet perspective, from which you can stop to identify how the various ideas presented resonate with you. Remember that the best gauge of the validity of any truth is not its scientific or academic substantiation, nor its popularity, but how it speaks to you on the level of your soul. So if you wish to draw the full potential and understanding from these words, I urge you to take your time and read thoughtfully as you wind your way down the path of these pages.

This book is what I found in answer to my question of how and why our universe works the way it does. I hope it may go some way towards answering the questions in your own heart and soul, whilst bringing us all closer to living in a world of peace, love and harmony.

Say not "I have found the truth," but rather,
"I have found a truth"

Say not "I have found the path of
the soul." Say rather, I have met the soul walking
upon my path."

For the soul walks upon all paths.
The soul walks not upon a line, neither does it grow
like a reed. The soul unfolds itself, like a lotus of
countless petals.

Kahlil Gibran

Within these two covers is the truth I have come across. This is the path upon which I have found the soul while out walking my experiences so far.

It is my hope that what I have found may become visible to you as you walk down this path.

It is my wish that you encounter the magic I have found with an open and questioning mind.

It is my desire that the words to follow reveal to you the true extent of your Godliness.

Part One

In the Beginning

In the beginning, there was one divine all-encompassing sphere of energy. This energy made up all that was – just as it still makes up all that is – and will continue to take up and make up all that will be in the time to come. Everything in existence is a part of this single energetic whole. This sphere of energy is every aspect of everything ever to have occurred and all that could ever occur in the future.

This omnipotent everything has been called different names by various groups of people throughout history. Eastern Taoists label it 'Tao', while followers of the Hindu faith choose the term 'Brahman'. Various Western metaphysicians and mystics favour the term 'God', 'God Energy' or 'The Universe'. My experience with this concept has taken place largely within the terminology of the Western world. As this is the terminology to which I am most accustomed, I will from this point on refer to this omnipotent sphere of all encompassing energy as God, or God Energy.

It is of vital importance that the distinction is made between the conventional idea of God that belongs to various religions and the God or God Energy to which I am now referring. Many religions, especially in the West, believe God to be a mystical man-like force that watches over our world, taking note of who does and does not adhere to his rules, and then dishing out or withholding his favours accordingly. This is not the God to which I refer. The God/God Energy is not a separate governing force, but rather the culmination of every scrap of energy that makes up our entire universe and all the wisdom, knowledge and experience found within it. For this reason, should it be difficult to distinguish between the two, I suggest readers replace the word God with whatever term better depicts this all-encompassing, omnipotent sphere of energy.

In the beginning, the God Energy was content in its existence, except for one thing – it had no experience of itself. It was the complete embodiment of perfection. It was the source and reservoir of all knowledge. It was the all-encompassing pool of wisdom. It was infinite abundance. But still the God Energy experienced a deficiency – it did not truly know itself. Because God was all that was, there was nothing against which it could compare itself. The perfection of the God Energy was meaningless without imperfection, just as we cannot have a perfectly formed blossom without many imperfect blossoms by which to measure it. God could not know the depth of its wisdom without some measure of ignorance, just as a gifted child is not gifted without ordinary peers. The God Energy's abundance was fruitless without the existence of lack, just as one person's wealth is only considered great when compared to another's poverty. The God Energy could not know itself for what it really was without some way of measuring what it was not.

As humans we are always learning about what and who we are through observation of that which surrounds us. But this option simply did not exist for God.

....

Stop and imagine for a moment that you are the only thing in existence. You are exactly who you are right now, except there is absolutely nothing else. The fact that nothing else exists does not change who you are, but how could you measure yourself without it? For instance, are you big or are you small? Right now you might be able to say, 'Yes, I'm a bit heavier than average,' or 'I'm tall,' or even 'I've got long black hair.' But if you were the only thing there was, would you still be a little heavy or tall or have long hair? In essence you would not have changed, but would you still be heavier if nobody was lighter? Would your hair still be long and black if there was no other hair? I suppose it would, but would it mean anything? This was the dilemma faced by God – it was everything, but what did that mean?

....

God had to devise a plan, another way in which to know itself. The only option left for God was to learn about itself through internal observation. It was for this purpose that our physical universe was created. With the manifestation of the universe, aspects of the God Energy chose to take on physical form. These pockets of energy chose to forget their Godly nature, so that they could experience themselves in relation to that which they thought to be separate from them. They chose to live within their illusion of separation so they could look at their surroundings and measure themselves experientially against them. Human life is no exception. We are God Energy manifest in physical form. We have taken on shape and purposely forgotten our true nature to experience the God Energy that is ourselves, in relation to the God Energy that is everything that surrounds us. We live our lives to experientially learn what we as individuals are, while simultaneously experiencing the God Energy that surrounds us. In this fashion, God is able to learn about itself through incremental experiences shared between tiny aspects of God Energy unaware of their Godly nature. Every experience we have is an experience had by God. Every time we learn something about ourselves, God learns something about itself. Every time we feel happy, God feels what it is like to smile. Every time we feel sad, God feels what it is like to cry.

Quite differently from what humankind often presumes, we are not the only form of life that embodies Godliness. God is everything and therefore everything with which we ever come into contact is an expression of the God Energy. We are no more or less important than anything else. A tiny bird flying past our window is as much God as we are, it is experiencing itself for exactly the same purpose as us. We would do well to remember that everything is God Energy and that everything is alive. Perhaps then we would begin to treat our surroundings with the respect they deserve. A stone skipping across a quiet watery pond is God Energy experiencing itself, as is the water in the pond and the air that the

God-stone glides through.

You, I and everything else are aspects of God Energy that believe ourselves to be individual entities adrift in a sea of foreignness. But this perception is an illusion, an illusion created so that God may learn about itself. In truth we are but aspects of the whole that surrounds us. We only experience feelings of individualism so we may experience ourselves against the God Energy that is all around us, for God, as God, whilst not knowing it. We are divinity manifest in physical form, the fingertips of Allah, the expression of God, the experience of Brahman. We are the Creator manifest.

....

Everything within our universe, although it may seem individual and separate, is in essence connected to everything else. You, I, the birds, the bees and the stars are all connected. We are all energy flowing and swirling in the omnipotent sphere of energy that is God. All that exists is this God Energy and as a result everything is intimately connected.

....

Collective Consciousness

Within the whole that is God, we find other smaller, more intimately connected pools of consciousness. These connections exist between aspects of God Energy that are manifest in like form. There consequently exists a close connection between all the individuals within a species that is not shared with an individual from another species. For example, all chimpanzees are connected through their web of collective consciousness on a deeper level than that which we as humans are connected to them. So too is all humankind connected on an intimate level, a level that is not shared with chimpanzees.

Evidence of the connection of species members is found throughout the natural world. Think of shoals of fish moving together with perfect synchronicity or flocks of birds darting this way or that like a single entity. An example I remember from my childhood took place at a dam not far from where I grew up. As we often did, my father and I were spending the day fishing. I remember my father excitedly pointing up into the clear blue sky at a pair of wattled cranes that came in to land alongside the dam. Being a bird lover, my dad was excited to see this pair of increasingly rare birds. Much to his delight, this was only the beginning and his excitement was about to soar to even greater heights. Over the course of the next few hours, spent on the water's edge, more and more cranes flew into view. Some of them arrived in pairs, some on their own and others in small groups. We watched spellbound as more and more of these rare birds came in from every direction to land in the area around the dam. When we eventually packed up and turned for home, we had counted over forty-two wattled cranes. Why all these birds decided to meet up on this particular day we did not know, but what perplexed us more was how they all knew exactly where to find each other?

We later found out through a friend who worked at the Parks Board that this was a flock of young birds meeting to pair off for mating. But the question of how they each knew where to meet and on which day was something that baffled me. I now understand that these cranes were each connected to one another on an intimate level, a level that allows them to communicate with each other telepathically. Just as we are connected to all other people, so too are chimpanzees connected to other chimpanzees and wattled cranes are connected to other wattled cranes.

This link joining each of us together exists almost entirely on a sub-conscious level. Although we generally are not aware of it, this bond provides the means through which we sub-consciously communicate amongst ourselves. Because of the ease with which we relate to the physical aspect of our existence, we often make the mistake of presuming that all of our communications occur on a physical level. While much of what we share is given and received in an aural or visible form, this is not the extent of our communications. The psychic aspects of our minds are always at work, sending and receiving information to and from our fellow species members. As these communications occur on a sub-conscious level, information shared in this way is not confined by the restrictions imposed upon communications carried out within the conscious aspects of our minds. Our collective consciousness allows information to be shared between all of us without us necessarily having to make any physical or verbal contact at all.

I conducted an experiment with one of my English classes in Taiwan while I was working on this concept. It was a small class of about twelve children between the ages of six and seven. At this point I had been teaching these children four times a week for several months and so we had begun to build up a good relationship and knew each other pretty well. In my schedule for the week I had eight or ten new vocabulary words to teach the class, but as they were a particularly bright and enthusiastic group they had already learned the vocabulary and we had some extra time to play games and have a little fun.

Being caught up with the idea of sub-conscious communication, I devised a new game, one that would become a favourite in the months to follow. To introduce this new idea I explained to the children that if I concentrated very hard on a word – one from our week's vocabulary – and if they were very, very quiet and concentrated very, very hard, they would be able to see what I was thinking and guess the word. I then held out the flash cards (picture-side out to the class) like a hand of playing cards and told everyone to concentrate really hard and made a big show of focusing and pretended to pull thoughts out of my head and throw them into the air above the children. At this point twelve hands would shoot up while little bottoms sprang from seats in excitement. The results of this game were absolutely astounding. Almost every time, the first child I chose got the word right, and if not, it was very rare for the game to go beyond two guesses. Because these young minds were still free of much of society's conditioning, they had not yet built up a mental wall that told them that they could not see my thoughts, so see my thoughts they did.

It is worth noting that we do not need to know each other well or be in close proximity to people to share information with them. In fact, information can be shared between individuals who have never met or heard of each other. In this way, we share information about every aspect of life and every possible view of it. Knowledge resulting from the experience of every individual is made accessible to the rest of us via this psychic web, thus allowing humankind to learn, albeit sub-consciously, from each other's experiences.

This long-distance anonymous sharing of information is visible when we look at how often inventors make the same discoveries or invent the same things either at the same time or shortly after each other. For example, in the 17th century at least three different mathematicians independently discovered calculus. Oxygen is another example. In the 18th century two different men discovered oxygen. The first lived in England and the second, who made the discovery a year later, lived in Sweden. And Alfred Russel Wallace and Charles Darwin both came up with the idea of evolution at approximately the same time! These individuals were unknowingly able to tune in to each other's thoughts, and as a result of being able to share information in this way, were able to come up with the same discoveries seemingly independently. Of course these famous inventors and scientists are not the only ones who have made use of this connection. Each and every one of us constantly receives and sends information in this way all the time.

Our collective consciousness resides within the realm of thought and it is through the act of thinking that we sub-consciously share information. We often presume our thoughts to be no more than a private internal monologue. But this is not the case. Each thought that we think travels far beyond the inner confines of our minds. When we think, our thoughts flow from the conscious level of our minds into the psychic level, from which they are quite literally broadcast to the world in the form of vibrating waves of thought energy. These thought waves surround us in every instant much like the invisible radio waves that flow from broadcasting towers. Similar to a broadcasting tower, each of us is constantly sending out our own signal in the form of millions of vibrating waves of thought energy. The thoughts that we broadcast are openly available to be interpreted by the psychic level of any other human mind, provided that it is operating on a similar frequency.

The frequency at which our psychic minds vibrate is determined by the nature of the thoughts we predominantly think. Each thought exists at a specific vibration, much like the different frequencies at which radio stations transmit their signals. Each station sends out its signal at a specific frequency so that all stations can transmit simultaneously without interfering with each other's transmissions. Similarly, our thoughts each vibrate at specific frequencies, determined by the nature of the thought. Thoughts of a similar nature vibrate at similar frequencies and thus within the same 'frequency range'. For example, thoughts of spiritual liberation all vibrate at similar frequencies, while thoughts of love or gardening vibrate within different frequency ranges. In this way, anyone thinking about a specific thing can sub-consciously identify similar thought waves and through doing this, access the information, held within the thoughts of others, that holds particular relevance to his or her situation.

An example of telepathically picking up information in this way happened to me a few months ago. I had left my home in the countryside and was on my way into town for an energy medicine session with my old Reiki master. There are two roads I could have taken to get to my appointment. One, the road I always took, was the slightly slower and longer route. The reason that I always took this route is that unlike the slightly faster highway, it did not require me to pay a toll, a fee disproportionately expensive seeing as though I was only going to travel on the highway for ten minutes and take the first off-ramp. On this particular occasion, for some unknown reason, I felt compelled to take the highway, a route I had up until then never taken for the short trip to town. When I arrived, a little early due to the abnormal route, my friend the practitioner was surprised to see me. She explained that there had been an accident on my usual route and the road was closed. Although I was not consciously aware of it at the time, I had sub-consciously picked up the thought energy of others and that prompted me to take the alternative road.

Our thoughts are therefore far from personal monologues of the internal mind, but instead are the means through which we readily communicate. Our thoughts are vibrating waves of information-saturated energy that travel effortlessly through time and space to be interpreted by others for whom the information is pertinent. Our minds pick up on like thought waves vibrating at similar frequencies to our own and so in this way we influence, and are influenced by, everyone operating at similar frequencies to ourselves. After all, there is truly only one mind, the mind of God, of which we are each a part. So what is really happening is that the God Mind is simply communicating within itself, much like the neurons in the brain that work together all the time.

....

When we peel an orange, we find that beneath the skin the fruit is made up of different segments. Should we bite into one of these segments we would find that they are made up of many small cells, each containing the juice of the orange. Similarly, should we take a closer look at the God Energy, we would see that it too is broken up into segments or closely connected pockets of energy. Humankind is one of these pockets. We, like the cells of the orange, are closely connected to each other as a result of all existing within the same pocket of energy, the same group within the whole that is God. This extra connection affords us the ability to subconsciously communicate with each other, to telepathically share information without any form of physical contact being made between the two parties. The way that we do this is through our thoughts. Our thought waves connect each of our minds and constantly share information between us without us ever realising it.

....

The Exchange of Information

Everything within this universe is God Energy actively experiencing itself through interactions with its surroundings. This means that humankind is not the only aspect of God that learns experientially. In fact, it is quite to the contrary. Every aspect of God Energy that is manifest in this physical plane is constantly learning from the interactions that it has with its surroundings. Whenever we come into contact with anything, it too is experiencing itself through the selfsame process. Although we seldom realise it, we interact with our surrounding environment on a multitude of different levels. Some of these interactions are physically based and as a result we are often aware of them. These physical interactions include talking to a friend, playing with a pet, tasting our food and feeling the wind blow against our skin. Moreover, at the same time as we carry out these physical interactions, a number of other energetic exchanges take place of which we are seldom aware.

We each inhabit energy bodies, the cores of which consist of dense matter in the shape of our physical forms. Surrounding our physical bodies we find our energy bodies, otherwise known as the electro-magnetic field or aura. Our aura is a sphere of fast (and therefore less dense) vibrating energy that is usually invisible to the human eye. What this means is that we extend beyond the physical bodies with which we so readily identify, with a bubble of personal energy reaching outwards as far as our limbs can extend. In the same way, everything around us consists of energy bodies of differing shapes and sizes. Whenever we are in close proximity to anything else, our auras can and do overlap without physical contact being made. In these instances, there is an automatic energetic exchange between the two energy fields and information can be shared from one to the other without us being conscious of what is happening. Information is thus swapped between our energy field and those that surround us on a constant basis, without us knowing.

A common example of the exchange of information through the overlapping of our energy fields is when we detect the presence of an object, animal or person without seeing, hearing or smelling them.

Have you ever been busy doing something when for no apparent reason you became aware of another person's presence in your vicinity? Perhaps you were in a public space where the presence of a stranger made you feel uneasy before you became consciously aware of him or her. Or perhaps you have felt the comforting feeling of a friend walking up to you before you turned around to say hello. We all interact this way. For the next few days try to become more aware of the information you sub-consciously pick up through your energy field. Every now and again quiet yourself down and try to detect what you can feel about your surroundings. It's amazing to see how much we absorb from our surroundings without realising it.

I learnt an interesting story from a man with whom I attended a workshop a little while ago. The day after the workshop I was standing in a queue waiting to watch a play when I noticed the man a few places ahead of me in the line. I was pleased when he recognised me and came over to introduce himself. During the workshop he had mentioned that he does a lot of work with the San Bushmen and Australian Aboriginal people, whose cultures have always fascinated me and I was keen to ask him more. We chatted for a couple of minutes while we waited to go into the theatre. He told me that he had some material I might like to read and so we set a time to meet up after the performance. While talking afterwards, the man told me the most fantastic story that beautifully illustrates how we exchange information with our surroundings. He told me about a friend of his, a white man who had spent many years living with the San Bushmen. While this man lived with the Bushmen he learned the ancient arts of tracking, and of reading the bush. He went on to tell me about a time he had gone walking in the bush with his friend the tracker. He told me how the tracker would periodically stop to touch the trunk of a tree or quietly look at the earth. On one particular instance the tracker placed his palm on a knotted old bark of a tree trunk and announced to his friend that further along the path was an antelope that was about to give birth. The men continued along the path and two hours later they came across the antelope trying to conceal her newborn in the bushes.

Just how the tracker learned to be so aware of what he was receiving from his surroundings I do not know. But this man was so aware of the exchange of information between his field of energy and those around him that he could tell exactly what was happening on the path two hours ahead of them.

While many energetic interactions occur as a result of physical proximity, they are not confined to our immediate surroundings. We also interact on a purely mental level. An example often used to illustrate mental interaction is that of coming into contact with someone who has been in our thoughts shortly before the contact is made, or intuitively knowing who is on the other end of a ringing telephone before we answer it. Remember that our thoughts contain information that is made accessible to others through the act of thinking. When we think of someone those thoughts become accessible to that person which often leads to a sort of telepathic contact being made between the two parties.

It is important for us to realise that no matter how basic a thing may seem to be, it too is experiencing an aspect of the God Energy through its interaction with us. Whilst we might experience feelings of enjoyment at looking out over a particularly beautiful view, that which makes up the scene before us experiences being the beauty that we behold. Be it trees in autumn colour, a flowing river or a rocky mountainside, it is all an aspect of God experiencing itself. In order to properly understand this concept, we need to remember that absolutely everything within our universe is God Energy and it is thus alive and intelligent. You, me, the trees, the river, the rocks and this book are all aspects of God Energy and we are all actively experiencing ourselves.

....

Though we generally see our world as a place of physical matter, a world of solids, liquids and gases, the truth is that, in essence, everything is energy vibrating at different speeds. This in turn means that you and I are not the physical beings we tend to think of ourselves as being, but rather energy bodies existing within a giant ball of God Energy. We are energy bodies living in a state of constant movement and flux. Energy cannot stagnate, it is always being exchanged between us and our surroundings. Though we see ourselves as separate entities interacting with each other, the truth is that we are each a part of the whole that is constantly interacting with itself through the shifting and flowing of God Energy.

....

Humankind's Creative Nature

Individual Reality

Due to the aspect of the God Energy that we as human beings represent, we have developed a tendency to presume ourselves to be special and superior to our surroundings. The principal reason for adopting this mindset is that humankind is the aspect of the God Energy that is responsible for the re-creation of our world. We are the God Energy that expresses the part of God that is creative. Due to the degree of control that this affords us, we often mistake our creative power for importance or rank over our surroundings, when in truth we are no better or worse, higher or lower than anything else. How could we be, when in essence we are all the same thing?

Ultimately we create on two levels, the first of which takes the form of our individual realities. It is the perception of many that life is a string of events that happen to us in a random and haphazard fashion. This could not be further from the truth. We are each responsible for the creation of our individual realities and we each attract to ourselves every event that makes up our lives. Those who are aware of this are able to make the most of their creative nature, while those ignorant to this truth are left to flounder confusedly in the unconscious creations of their minds and souls. The key to unleashing the full potential of our creative ability lies in properly understanding the process of creation. That is, understanding the three different manners in which we create and merging them together for a single unified purpose.

We as humans are made up of three aspects of self, namely the body, mind and spirit, the details of which we shall go into later in the book. It is fitting that we create on three different levels.

Firstly we create from the body in a tactile physical form. This could be anything from painting the Mona Lisa to building a house or making a sandwich.

Secondly we create on a more abstract level using the mind. It is through our seemingly unique spectrum of thought that we create through the mind. No thought is idle or meaningless. Every thought is powered by creative energy. In fact, we could go so far as to say that the process of thinking is synonymous with creation. When we think, what we are doing is empowering the subject of our thoughts with energy; the subject then begins to leave the abstract realm of thought and moves towards becoming a reality. In other words, when we think, for example of love, we empower love with creative energy and begin attracting it into our lives. Thirdly, we create from the level of the soul. Within each of us resides the soul or higher self. This is the part of you or me that sees through the illusion that is our world. The soul is the part of us that knows the truth of our existence – the truth that we are all intimately connected to one another – that All is One and All is God. It is from this higher self, this sliver of Godliness at the very core of our being that we do the most powerful creation. It is from the soul that we have the ability to change our world in the most profound and magical fashion.

It is fairly easy to see and understand how we create using our hands and bodies on a physical level. But the process of creation belonging to the mind is often confused and misunderstood. As mentioned, our minds create through the thoughts they generate. All thought is powered with creative energy that brings the subject of the thoughts towards physical manifestation.

Not all of our thoughts become real. We think many seemingly random thoughts all the time – small and abstract thoughts that never make it through to becoming a physical reality. For instance, when we read a book, a story about another time and place captures our mind. But no matter how much we think about the story or how real the experience of reading the book may be, we do not physically manifest the situation from the book into our reality. In other words, if I read Alice in Wonderland, I do not find myself slipping down the rabbit hole or sipping tea with the Mad Hatter. This is because we have a sort of filtration system that sifts through our thoughts and only manifests the bigger picture.

This system works in two ways. Firstly, there exists a delay between the thoughts we think and their manifestation, and secondly, how often and how passionately we think about a thing determines whether or not it will become a physical reality.

The more frequently and passionately we think of an event or object, the more creative energy there is behind its manifestation and the more likely it is to become a reality. We could get excited about something once, and it would not become physically manifest, or we could think about something all the time, but have no passion behind the thoughts and this also would not become manifest in our lives. I have experienced this many times with regard to money and business. Over the past few years I have tried a number of small business ideas to make money. I have dabbled in sculpture, practiced Reiki, made corporate key rings, and even done some building restoration. Each time I got excited about an idea, I poured my creative thought energy into it in the form of constant, passionate thought. Each time things would go well for a few months. I would be booked up with Reiki clients, my sculptures would sell or I would get orders for key rings. Then as I gradually realised that I had no deep interest in what the business did and stopped thinking about it so determinedly, it would decline and I would be forced to abandon the idea and go searching for something new. It is the combination of passion and regularity that creates our realities and it was the lack of these that led to my business ideas going down the tubes.

As with any expression, it is important to understand exactly what is meant by 'passionate thinking'. The passion to which I refer is not necessarily the romantic intensity often related to matters of love and happiness; it also includes the negative intensity related to emotions such as fear, anxiety and hatred. It is not only our most positive thoughts that manifest into reality but also their negative counterparts.

The quality (positivity or negativity) of our thinking – conscious or not – is directly parallel to the quality of the experience we manifest. Thoughts of a positive nature manifest positive experiences, whilst negative thoughts manifest negative experiences. Negative thoughts of wanting and lack create experiences of wanting and lack, whilst thoughts of gratitude create experiences of fulfilment and enjoyment. In other words, it is not enough to think of how much we want something in order to manifest the experience of having it. What we need to do is think thoughts that are synonymous with already possessing that which we desire and then we will call the experience of having what we want towards ourselves. Affirmations, such as the 'gratitude' that my wife and I used in the example of our Taiwanese home are a powerful tool for ensuring that our thoughts are geared towards having and not wanting. By changing the format of I want – into I am so grateful for – we automatically start sending the right message out into the cosmos. We begin sending out the sort of message that will call our desires towards us, instead of pushing them away.

A family of friends who recently immigrated to New Zealand told me a delightful story that illustrates how using positive thought can create the fulfilment of our desires. When the family (father, mother, daughter of eleven and son of six) arrived in New Zealand there was much talk and excitement about what sort of car they should buy. Each family member had their own prerequisites for the vehicle and each seemed totally incongruous with the others. The mother decided that the car needed to be safe and spacious. The father declared jokingly that he wanted a sports car. The daughter decided she wanted a fancy interior. She and her brother were desperate for a car with a GPS. The mother on the other hand was against a GPS because she felt it would weaken their natural navigational instincts. Also they wanted to spend around

NZ$10,000. With this long list of requirements in mind, they set out in search of the perfect vehicle. At this point I should mention that I know that the family is very aware of how we create through our thinking and the need for positive thinking. When they visited the car dealer one particular vehicle caught their eye straight away. When they climbed inside to take a closer look, the father turned on the radio and his favourite song was playing (synchronicity is worth noting). As they inspected the car they noticed that it was kitted out with air bags and all the safety trimmings. As well as this, the seats all folded neatly away to create extra space whenever required. The interior was very smart with leather upholstery and a shiny wooden steering wheel, just as prescribed by the daughter, but what made her and her brother even happier was the built-in GPS. To the mother's delight, it turned out that the GPS was entirely in Japanese and therefore of no practical use at all. As far as the sports car goes, the vehicle turned out to have golden mag wheels, which made the father chuckle. What is more, the car cost NZ$9,990, ten dollars less than what they hoped to spend. It is worth mentioning that they have since seen the same sort of car for almost half the price. As the mother said to me, 'One must be careful what one wishes for.'

Although positive thought is such an important tool, it is frequently misunderstood. We often see people battling to make the distinction between positive and negative thinking, especially when it comes to the materialistic side of life. I have a friend who, despite being spiritually aware, really battles with this. She goes through life thinking about what she wants from a negative perspective, in other words, thinking of how these things are missing in her life and how badly she wants them. She enters every competition that comes her way and tries every good-luck gimmick out there, but year in and year out her situation remains dire. She sadly does not seem to be able to realise that it is her passion that is stopping her from getting what she wants. Because she WANTS so badly she constantly affirms to the rest of the universe that she does not have what she wants, and so continues to create the same situation of not having for herself. This friend also provides a good example of someone who, despite being spiritually aware and knowledgeable, has not managed to merge her mind and spirit with her body and therefore does not associate with it or the physical world in a very positive fashion.

The importance of merging the body, mind and spirit is paramount to anyone who wants to lead a harmonious life. An effective way to go about doing this (which we do go into later in this chapter) is through daily practice of a spiritual art.

Then there is another sort of person, someone who uses his or her passion in a positive way and always seems to get what he or she wants. These people look at life and see what they DO have and how much they DO get. Because of this outlook and their prior success, they throw out positive, 'I will get what I want, because look how lucky I always am' thoughts. As a result they create the experience of fulfilling their desires and do actually get what they want. We would all do well to be aware of the sort of passion we display as its nature determines whether we will succeed or fail in our endeavours.

When dealing with the creations of the mind it is worth noting that thought seldom travels alone. We do not think in isolated individual thoughts. Instead, we tend to think within larger thought patterns. These patterns of thought are essentially the grouping of like thoughts, categorised by either their subject or nature. These thought patterns are often affiliated with companion emotions that help us to recognize them. For example, when we are concerned about something, say a dwindling bank account, feelings of anxiety and worry alert us to the fact that we are thinking about it, rather than noticing the actual thoughts themselves. In the same way, when we fall in love, we are not necessarily aware that we are thinking about our loved one but our joy shows us that we are. With this in mind, we can learn to use our emotions as signposts or checkpoints to ensure that we are happy with our hidden trains of thought. When we experience negative emotions like anger, fear and anxiety on a regular basis, we learn that we have a negative thought pattern going around in our mind. This then gives us the opportunity to rectify our approach towards whatever it is that is bothering us, and change it from a negatively based approach into one geared towards creating the situation we want.

Something that we often take for granted is how much our thought patterns are influenced by our surroundings and the people closest to us. We absorb most of our ideas about life, including how it can and should be lived, from our general environment. As a result, we often find ourselves thinking and acting in a manner similar to those around us. We tend to accept popular ideas without first weighing up their validity, and in so doing, find ourselves in danger of leading lives that mimic the average life of our average peer.

When we are younger, we tend to absorb the predominant thought patterns of our parents. If they think life is a struggle and money is hard to come by, then more often than not, so do we. If they discriminate racially against this group or that, we tend to think their discrimination is valid. And if they lead with a loving and compassionate example, then we learn to see the world as a happy place full of good things.

However, it is not only as children that we adopt the thought patterns of those around us. As adults, our friends, spouses and colleagues drastically affect our outlook on the world. It is important that we do not blindly adopt the attitudes and thought patterns of those around us without thinking for ourselves. So often we see people adopting each other's ideas about life without first weighing them up for themselves. Just because our spouse thinks that there is not enough money to go around does not mean we have to mirror his fear. Just because a work colleague dislikes her job it does not mean that we should, and just because a friend gets worked up about the political situation, it does not mean we need to echo that stress in our lives.

Recently I was in the company of a group of friends when the gloomy topic of hijackings came up. Hijacking is a common occurrence in some areas of South Africa, where I live. Accordingly, it is an unfortunate preoccupation of many people who talk and think about it all the time. Remember, as we think, so shall it be. As I was fond of the people with whom I was sitting, I did not want to get up and leave the table. But I was also aware that I did not want to sit there and absorb their negative views of the world. Being aware of the negative influences of the conversation I was able to make a conscious decision to change the topic. Had I not been aware of the effects of their views on my psyche, I may have sat there quietly listening to all the horrible stories and complaints. By doing so I would probably have left feeling uneasy and expecting a robber to jump out at every stop on the way home. Of course, as our thoughts and expectations create our realities, I would have been doing myself a big disfavour.

Some good news for those of us looking to turn our lives from the conditioned norm to the experiences we desire, is that conscious thought holds within it more creative energy than subconscious thought. What this means is that manifestations created from conscious thought easily replace those created from sub-conscious mutterings. Therefore, by consciously focusing our thoughts (in a positive way) upon that which we desire, we can replace our conditioned thought patterns with whatever we choose to create in their place. In the example of my Taiwanese experience, our conscious effort to create feelings of gratitude towards the sort of home that we wanted were powerful enough to override our previous assumption that we would end up in a cramped one-roomed flat.

While the creative power of our thinking is a hugely powerful tool in the creation of our realities, we may well come across instances where – though we are doing everything 'right' – we just are not getting the results we desire. In these instances it is important to remember that the creative ability of the soul dwarfs that of the mind. It may happen that though we feel that we know what is best for us, the soul has a preferred path lined up for us to experience what we need to experience at the time.

This brings us back to our third and most powerful form of creation – creations stemming from the soul. Unlike the ever-uncertain mind, the soul has only one desire, which is to once again be knowingly merged with the God Energy, to transcend the illusion of separation and achieve for the mind and body what the Buddhist faith calls enlightenment. It constantly creates a reality around itself that puts it (us) nearest to the realisation of enlightenment. This does not mean that our soul is going to keep manifesting the walls of an ashram around us as we go about trying to live our lives. Remember that we are here to feel the full spectrum of experience that is life, enlightenment simply being the last of these. Our soul, knowing the intimate truth about our existence, creates the experiences we need to embody on our way there. It calls into being the best possible situations for us to experience the experiences we most need at any one time.

The trouble is that most of us do not know that our higher self is constantly giving us what we need at every corner, straight, incline and downhill of our spiritual path. The reason that we are so unaware of this is that each of our three aspects of self have drifted apart from each other and are trying in vain to create independently of the other two. If we really want to master our creative ability, we need to re-merge the body, mind and spirit to combine their creative potential for a single purpose or direction.

A great way to do this is through daily spiritual practice. I first became aware of this when Claire and I moved back to Taiwan for a second bout of English teaching. Soon after arriving we became friendly with one of my wife's co-workers, who turned out to be an amazing yoga teacher. To cut a long story short, after repeated requests from my wife, our friend started up a small yoga class on the top floor of our house. Slightly reluctantly I bought myself a yoga mat and dragged my feet up the stairs for our first class. Within an hour I was sold. It turned out that our friend teaches a form of Hatha Yoga which is much slower moving than the other form of yoga that I had done before. Furthermore, she teaches from a quiet and spiritual perspective, unlike the more fitness-oriented classes that I had previously attended. Within a couple of months I had fallen so much in love with this form of yoga that I began getting up earlier before work to start my day with a yoga session.

As time went by and I became more serious about my daily practice, I began to become aware of the profound effect it was having on my life. I found that I was becoming a much more balanced person, living life from a calmer and more spiritually intuitive and harmonious perspective. After some reflection I realised that the reason for this was that, through my practice, I was achieving better balance between my body, mind and spirit.

Of course, while Hatha Yoga is what worked for me, it would not work for everyone. The trick to creating a daily spiritual practice that brings into balance the body, mind and soul, is to find a form of spiritual art that best suits us. It could be yoga, meditation, Qi Gong, Sufi Dancing, Shamanic Shaking or any of countless other forms. In my case, it just happened to be that particular form of Hatha Yoga that gave me what I needed at that particular time. It is worth mentioning that, though I still do practice this yoga, I have found that different spiritual arts suit me at different times. It is quite plausible for us to chop and change between different mediums depending upon where we are in our lives. The beauty is that there are as many spiritual arts and teachers out there as there are different sorts of people, so no matter what our situation, there will be an art perfectly suited to our needs.

The trick to finding the spiritual art that best suits us is the use of our intention. I remember about a week before that first yoga session, saying to my wife that I felt ready for a fresh new spiritual path and intended to find a teacher to lead me down it. Within no time our Yogi appeared.

....

If you are trying to find a spiritual art that suits you, simply intend that it comes across your path and see what comes up. Follow your intuition and keep your eyes open as – be it straight away or in a few days, weeks or months – the right path will find you at the right time.
....

Though I loved the Hatha Yoga right from the first session, doing a spiritual practice is not always easy and fun. If our spiritual art becomes too easy, we are probably not engaging with it and may simply be going through the motions. Spiritual practice is challenging. That is the whole point – to challenge the unbalanced way we live life and begin to see through the illusion that we work so hard to uphold. We have to be prepared to put in time and effort to reap the rewards of our practice. I like to think of my daily practice as similar to learning a language. No one expects to be fluent in Russian after two or three hours of practice, not to mention two or three months or even years. We quite happily accept that if we want to speak a new language we need to put in constant time and energy. The same applies with our spiritual practice. Luckily for us, much like the immense rewards of being able to conduct more and more of our lives in a new language, the spiritual rewards generated from a daily practice are well worth the effort.

Another thing that I learned from the adoption of my yoga practice is the importance of a teacher. Were it not for our friend, there is no way that I could have gotten as deeply into yoga as I have. In this there really is no substitute for human interaction – a book or DVD simply cannot give what a teacher standing infront of us can. That is not to say that, should we not be able to find a teacher, we should not attempt the practice ourselves, but it is definitely worth bearing in mind that a teacher is an invaluable tool to anyone wanting to forge a new spiritual practice. Similarly, I would highly recommend finding a spiritual art that already exists rather than trying to create our own from scratch. I have seen movies and read books where monks meditate through the acts of sweeping or scrubbing floors. In fact I recently met a Buddhist man who practices meditation through the brewing of coffee. I can almost guarantee that the sweeping monks and coffee-man started off practicing a standard system, tried and tested over generations. Only when they became practised at their spiritual art were they able to transfer it to their daily chores. Washing the dishes can be a spiritual art but we should not fool ourselves into using it as an excuse not to do our daily practice. I have done this and it does not work!

Something else that I have come to realise about daily spiritual practice is that part of the benefit that is derived is from the routine of the practice and not the motions alone. What I mean by this is that though the actual asanas (poses) and pranayama (breath work) of my yoga practice stimulate my body and energy body as well as calming my mind, the very act of making time for my practice every day (because of its spiritual importance to me) sends out a message that my spiritual self is of great importance, thus giving it the space to flourish and grow.

This book is full of ideas and philosophies, words and sentences about how our world works on a deep and mysterious level. These words, no matter how intellectually stimulating they may be, hold little worth should they remain only words and ideas.

In order to derive true benefit from this book you need to cross the threshold of the mind and transform this information into knowledge, experience and understanding within all three aspects of yourself. The way to go about integrating this information into experience and understanding is by the merging of the body, mind and spirit through your daily spiritual practice.

Everything within our universe is God Energy experiencing an aspect of God. Every experience had by anything, be it a person, a fish, a tree or a rock, is an experience had by God. Humankind is the aspect of God Energy that represents the creative nature of God. Though we are seldom aware of it, we are each responsible for the creation of every event in our lives. We quite literally create our worlds around us all the time. The manner in which we do this is firstly through the divine organising power of the soul and then through our thoughts and actions. Some people have difficulty understanding this, as they cannot fathom the cosmos shifting to create their individual worlds as their innermost desires and thought prescribes. What they are forgetting is that All is One. When the cosmos shifts to create our reality around us, it too is creating its reality around itself. Remember that everything is one and that we are intimately connected to everything there is, so what we want is what the cosmos wants. All that is standing between us and anything we desire is a communication barrier between our body, mind and soul. All we need to do to break through this is to find the spiritual art that best suits us and let it transform us with our daily practice.

Collective Reality

The second form of reality, for which each of us is responsible, is our global or collective reality. Just as our thoughts create within our individual realities, so does our collective thinking create on a shared level. When we think, our thoughts are pooled in a collective human mind. Similar to how our individual minds create, our collective mind is responsible for the manifestation of a collective reality in which we all share.

Our collective consciousness, being the culmination of all thought, is charged with the creative energy that empowers the thoughts of which it is comprised.

Every natural phenomenon that in any way affects humankind is the direct result of our collective psyche. This is not to say that without people the Earth would stop spinning and volcanoes would stop erupting. But what it does mean is that every time we experience a natural catastrophe, its effect on us is determined by our collective psyche. Therefore, when a tsunami annihilates entire communities, it does so because of our collective psyche and our collective thinking. Of course the same holds true every time a good spring rain or a sunny summer's day makes crops grow and produces food for us all.

I recently read an article by a successful, yet seemingly angry, Body, Mind, Spirit author. He was annoyed and disillusioned with all the authors out there putting forward the idea that we each create our own realities. The reason he had such difficulty understanding this, is that he, along with many others, could not understand why there are so many people born into dire situations. He said that he could not believe each of us creates our own realities when there are so many people living lives of misery and misfortune, for example, the millions of AIDS orphans in sub-Saharan Africa. He posed the question, 'If we each create our own realities, why do so many people choose to live lives of hardship and suffering?'

The answer to this question is found in the creation of our collective reality.

Seth Falconer

Our collective psyche dictates the quality of life into which each of us is born, in a proportionate fashion. In other words, the more people thinking within miserable thought patterns, the more creative energy there is behind misery and the higher the proportion of miserable existences into which children are born. The sum total of new lives started through the birth of our babies is, therefore, proportionately divided up into the amount of positive creative energy available, which creates positive starts for the children, and negative creative energy, which creates tough beginnings for the newborns. Of course where and when we are born does not dictate the remainder of our lives. As we already know, our surroundings influence the way we think, especially when we are young. This means, children born into difficult situations often lack an example, or the tutelage, to enable them to create their lives to be whatever they desire. As a result the odds are stacked against them and it remains difficult for them to break the chain of hardship into which they are born.

In order to properly understand this we have to view humankind as a complete unit. Just as the proportion of uplifting thoughts we think affects the number of uplifting circumstances in our lives, so too does this work on a collective level. It is not a matter of vindictive behaviour towards one aspect of humankind and favouritism towards another. Each and every one of us represents an aspect of the collective whole, the whole that we all contribute towards creating. So when we begin life, we do so in a way that best represents the collective psyche of the time. Sadly for many, this means starting out with a rough deal. This provides yet another reason to carefully monitor our thoughts and ensure that we are putting out as much positive energy as possible. The most effective way to do this is to bring our mind into harmony with our body and soul. When the mind is in balance with the body and soul, it will automatically begin adapting its ways to suit that of the soul, and in so doing, begin working towards harmony and enlightenment for one and all. Again, this underlines the importance of a spiritual practice aimed at achieving this synchronisation.

An interesting example of how our thinking affects our surroundings on a collective level comes from the experiments done by the Japanese scientist, Dr Masaru Emoto[1]. Dr Emoto is famous for his experiments showcasing the effects of our thoughts, words and attitudes on water. He exposes water samples to a number of different stimuli – sometimes speech, sometimes written words, pictures, music and so on. He then freezes the samples and takes photographs of them through a high-powered microscope. The results are phenomenal. Water samples exposed to negative stimuli make deformed, grotesque crystals, while those exposed to positive stimuli create beautifully-formed crystals. Emoto then took his experiments a step further. With the help of a Buddhist monk, he conducted an experiment on a polluted lake in Japan. Dr Emoto first photographed the polluted water, which formed crude, ugly crystals. After the monk blessed the lake and spent some time conducting a healing prayer on its banks, Emoto took a second set of samples to find that the blessed lake water formed beautiful symmetrical crystals. This provides us with a glimpse of how our thoughts, words and actions affect our shared surroundings.

So, the thoughts we think affect the creation of our individual realities while at the same time becoming part of the pool of thought that is our collective reality. As a result, our collective reality is the grouping of all of the characteristics of all of our individual realities. Similarly, our predominant thought patterns play a large role in the creation of our individual worlds; the predominant traits of our individual realities affect the manifestation of our collective world. The end result is a world that depicts the principal characteristics of our individual realities. Accordingly, the more anger, prejudice and hatred expressed in our individual lives, the more war, famine and injustice we create on a global level. Conversely of course, the more compassion, love and understanding we create in our individual lives, the more healing, love and health we create for the globe.

In a world where everything is intimately connected to everything else, our actions logically affect more than ourselves alone. When we think, not only do our thoughts create within our individual reality, but they are also pooled in the immense reservoir that is the human psyche. The collective human mind creates a collective world that affects each and every one of us as well as all that surrounds us. Therefore, you and I are not only responsible for the quality of our personal lives but also the quality of life of everyone and everything that surrounds us. Whenever we transmit positive thoughts into the ether we are not only uplifting our individual experiences, but also those of everyone and everything else. Conversely, our negative thinking can and does drag everyone else down with us, as the effects of our thoughts ripple through the pool of the collective human mind.

The Relationship between Individual and Collective Reality

While our collective reality is something in which we all share, it is not something that we all experience in the same way. The scope for experience that we each have is determined by our apparent individuality. In other words, we only experience a small part of the diverse collective reality on offer. This is why two different people can experience totally different things from the same field of potentiality. For example, take a monk living a completely spiritual existence high in the mountains of Tibet. The experiences of this monk seem entirely different from those of a busy accountant living in any major city across the globe. The reason that these two people have such different experiences is that they are each accessing different aspects of the potential on offer within our collective reality. It is as though we live our lives looking through a pair of binoculars. What we see is high-detail and crisp, yet it is only a small portion of the full view that lies before us.

No matter whether we are the monk sitting in deep meditation, or the accountant controlling the funds of a major corporation, there are trends of our collective reality that we cannot escape experiencing in one way or another.

The prevailing attitudes of our collective consciousness affect each and every one of us, and the vehicle through which these prevailing attitudes travel is our societies. From the very beginning the societies into which we are born mould the way in which we develop. We are brought up within social orders that govern the way in which our role models think and act and, accordingly, we almost always absorb the beliefs and ideas of those who raise us. In other words, the attitudes of the culture within which we grow up become our initial way of thinking and thus our initial approach to life.

This leads to us creating personal realities that mimic our larger society. Our societies condition our thinking, which then influences the nature of our personal realities. These conditioned thoughts then contribute to the future creation of a collective reality that is much the same as the one that came before it. So, in this way our individual and collective realities are locked in a cycle of interdependence and influence. Our global reality influences the way we think about that which surrounds us, which in turn leads to the creation of our worlds, individual and then global, in the image of the suggestions we receive from our collective worldview.

For instance, our society suggests to us that we need to work hard at our jobs, whether we like them or not. It suggests that we need the security of the monthly salary to survive. How many people do we know who slog away, day and night, at jobs they do not like because society tells them that it is far too dangerous to follow their hearts? Each time any of us conforms to the idea that work is not supposed to be fun and that we must plough ahead no matter what, these ideas are re-fed into the collective reality and our society continues to give us this message.

Therefore, the thinkers responsible for thinking the thoughts that colour our world are held back by the influence that our previous thoughts had upon the world that will, in turn, influence our further thinking. Our experiences of the global reality today affect the creation of our personal reality tomorrow, which then contributes to creating a future global reality that is similar to the one that initially influenced us.

We create our own realities, through our thoughts, which are charged with creative power and when this power is grouped together in pockets of like-minded thoughts, they literally create the events that make up our lives. We have learned that our reactions to the situations we have previously called into being are the channel through which we can change our future experiences. By choosing to replace old negative response mechanisms we can replace fear with joy and hatred with love.

This chapter has also shown us how we create on two different levels. Our creative nature creates our individual lives, as well as contributing to a global reality in which we all share. Not only are we responsible for our individual realities, but so too are we collectively responsible for the state of our Earth and everything that happens upon her. We have seen how our thoughts travel beyond our individual lives and influence everyone else, how our negative thought patterns not only hamper us individually, but also drag down the consciousness of the rest of the globe. However, we now know that whenever we make a change for good within our individual lives, that change is mirrored within the collective world and helps to raise the global consciousness.

Finally, this chapter highlights the cycle in which our individual and collective realities are locked. Like a dog chasing its tail, our individual worlds follow the image of our collective reality. Ironically, it was our individual realities that created the collective reality in the first place. We would all do well to make sure that what we choose to create within our personal realities is not simply what our collective world is suggesting to us through the attitudes and actions of our global society, but what we choose for ourselves.

All is One

If our collective reality were to have a face, it would be our global society. If it were to have a voice, it would be our media with its suggestions on how life should be lived and the handed-down philosophies from bygone eras. Though we may like to think otherwise, the voice of our collective world reaches out to each and every one of us. Its insistent murmurs invariably affect the way we see the world around us. This influence upon our thoughts and attitudes naturally affects the future creation of our individual realities in the image of the suggestions whispered into our ears.

The irony is that while our collective world influences our individual realities, it is totally reliant upon them for its existence as our individual worlds are the building blocks from which it is forged. What came first, the chicken or the egg, the collective or individual reality? Who can tell? But, what we do know is that our two forms of reality are locked in a perpetual cycle of interdependence and influence.

"Be aware of what you receive from your surroundings and be mindful of what you think in response as your thoughts affect not only your life, but the existence of everyone and everything else".

Re-creation

We tend to see life as a continuous flowing experience, slowly developing with time and space. Because of this perception of fluidity, we generally presume the reality within which we live to be an evolving concern that grows and changes with time. Nevertheless, this perception is flawed. Even though our realities seem to evolve, the truth is that we re-create them afresh all the time.

In our defence, it is not without good reason that we mistake reality to be evolving. When we look at the realities that we previously created, we can easily see how one could presume history to have been made up of a single reality, changing over time. After all, each of our realities so far has looked and acted remarkably like those that came before them. The reason we keep creating realties that look and act the same, is that the thoughts we use to colour our realities are thought whilst experiencing the previous reality. As we already know, our thoughts create, but the effect of their creation is not instantaneous. There exists a time lapse between thought and manifestation. As a result, our experiences are not the manifestation of current thinking, but rather of prior thought.

This lapse between thought and manifestation becomes evident when we look at the creative effectiveness of our thinking within other realms of existence. When we dream, our consciousness leaves this physical realm and enters the realm of dreaming. The defining parameters of this dream world are not the same as those of our waking world. In the dream realm there is no time or physicality. As a result, there is no gap between our thoughts and their manifestations. This is why, when we dream, our surroundings are constantly replaced at the drop of a thought. Why one moment we can be licking an ice cream on the beach with our grandmother and the next be held captive in a spaceship headed for Mars.

Due to the absence of time, we can experience dreams that feel as though they took place over a long period, in what would have only been an instant in our waking world. When we dream, each train of thought creates a situation that we experience until we think of something else. This new chain of thought then causes our situation to be re-created and so our surroundings immediately change. If we permanently lived within the realm of dreaming, our creative nature would soon become apparent because there the effects of our thinking are instantly visible. Due to the fact that we primarily reside within this physical realm, our perception is conditioned by our experience of the time lapse between thought and manifestation. This is why most of us have not yet been able to make the mental correlation between thought and its corresponding manifestation.

We live in an environment created from our previous thinking, thinking that was conditioned by our prior experiences. We then create our future realities from present moment situations, situations that influence our thinking now and therefore our future creation. As a result of this, we re-create realities that look and act much the same as those that came before them, and in doing this we continue the perception of reality as fluid and evolving.

The knowledge that our realities are completely re-created and therefore do not evolve is of particular significance to those of us interested in changing the experiences we have in our individual and collective worlds. The key to bringing about the change we want to see is to become aware of and alter our reactions to the events and circumstances that make up our lives. What we sometimes seem to forget is that absolutely every action we take is the result of a choice to act. The reason we seem to forget this is the reflex nature from which we carry out so many of our daily activities. The experience of learning to ride a bicycle illustrates this point well.

Do you remember learning to ride a bike? When you first climbed on the bike, everything about the experience would have been new and would have required a lot of conscious effort to perfect. For instance, you would have needed to make a conscious effort to keep your balance, you would have had to remember to keep peddling if you wanted to continue moving, and you would have had to think about pulling in the brakes when you wanted to stop. Over time, with practice, you probably became familiar with the bicycle and these basic actions would have become what we often term 'second nature'. In other words, you probably no longer need to consciously think about pulling in the brakes when you want to slow down, or peddling harder when you want to speed up. What has happened here is that, with practice, you have become accustomed to riding the bicycle and as a result, your thoughts and actions have become automatic and sub-conscious.

It is worth noting that although these thoughts may now be sub-conscious, they still occur and although you may not be conscious of them, when you ride a bike today, you are still deciding to apply the brakes or peddle faster.

The relevance of this example, of a shift of thinking from conscious to sub-conscious thought, is not confined to the physical actions that we regularly perform. We each have sub-conscious, pre-programmed reaction processes that we apply to all aspects of life. It is important to remember that we created these response mechanisms based upon our previous experiences, experiences had in the realities that we previously created. Therefore, we judge our surroundings and determine what reactions to take, based upon experiences from past realities, realities that are separate from the present moment.

We expect the present moment to act the same way that our previous realities did, and as a result of this predictive thinking, we re-create the present reality in the image of its predecessor. Of course our realities need not continue to act the same. Through becoming conscious of our reactions, we can break this chain of repetitive creation. We can stop carrying forward the traits of the present that we do not like and instead replace them with whatever we choose.

The difficulty is that because of the time lag between thought and manifestation, we need to change our reactive thinking in the present, for the future. We have to consciously monitor our reactions whilst still experiencing the situations that we wish to change.

We cannot direct the wind but we can adjust our sails.
Bertha Calloway

Whilst in truth we have directed the winds that blow through our lives, we cannot change their course in the instant that they pass through. When these metaphorical winds blow, we cannot alter their paths. We have already set them on their course.

What we can do is to react to these events in such a way as to ensure the future creation of situations that better suit us. In so doing, we can set our metaphorical sails to allow the wind to carry us to wherever it is that we want to be. What is important in the present is not the circumstances that make up the moment, but rather how we react to them. We cannot change events as they unfold before us but we can decide upon our reactions to them. If we are deliberate and mindful in our reactions, we can re-create our world into whatever we choose.

There is an Indian fable which embodies this concept beautifully. The story is set in rural India just after the marriage of a young woman to the man she loves. Unfortunately for the bride, her mother-in-law is a bitter old woman who thought that nobody was good enough for her son, especially not his new wife. According to custom in the area, the young woman moves into her husband's family home where she is to live side by side with her tyrannical mother-in-law. After a few months, the young wife is 'driven mad' by the old woman's bitterness. Out of desperation, she turns to a local hermit renowned for his wisdom. She tells the wise old man about her mother-in-law and the terrible things she is doing to her. Sobbing, she begs him for help.

The old man produces a small glass vial filled with a transparent liquid. He instructs the young woman to put a drop of the clear liquid into her mother-in-law's food every night. He tells her that the liquid within the bottle is a powerful poison that will kill the old woman slowly over the coming weeks. He explains that the poison works in such a way that it will look like she has died of natural causes.

Feeling buoyed up by the wise man's support, the young woman returns home. Each night she puts a drop of the liquid into her mother-in-law's food and waits patiently for her to become ill and die. Knowing that the old woman would soon be gone, the young wife becomes more compassionate and friendly towards her. When the mother-in-law shouts at her or calls her names, she simply smiles and does as she is asked. In response to the small acts of kindness displayed by the young woman, the mother-in-law slowly begins to change. She no longer shouts as much or accuses the young woman of as much wrongdoing and stops calling her hurtful names. In fact once, after the young wife gently holds her arm as they walk through the local market, the old woman even apologises for her cruel behaviour.

The next day the young woman rushes to the hermit, once again weeping. She tells the old man that she no longer wants to kill her mother-in-law. The wife begs and begs him for some sort of a potion to reverse the poison she has been feeding her. With a smile the wise old man tells her that there will be no need for such a thing. He explains to her that the vial he has given her is not poison but only water. The old man had never intended the young woman to kill her mother-in-law. He knows that by helping her to change her reaction to the situation, she will be able to re-create their relationship into something better.

If we are compassionate when faced with bitterness, then we create good will. If we are grateful for what we have when faced with lack, then we bring about more abundance. If we find a reason for joy when faced with despair, we create more happiness. But if we give in to our old reaction mechanisms and react negatively, then we attract negative situations to make up our future.

When next you are faced with a situation that displeases you, try not to give in to feeling angry or sad. Rather choose to act positively and in so doing change your situation for the better. For instance, if you are having trouble with your boss at work, try not to feel angry and upset about him; focus your energy on aspects of your work that you do like. It is always a good idea to start by writing down a list of things for which you are grateful, things that you already have. Then, when you have your attention focused on the good things in your life, start writing down what you want that you do not yet have. Remember that it is vital that you keep it in a 'gratitude-based' format. A list of I wants will only create a situation of wanting and what you are after is the experience of having. If your boss bothers you, it would be a good idea to write down what you would like from your boss. If he is a rude person, and you would prefer someone kinder and more caring you could write something like: I am so grateful for such a kind and compassionate boss. Then every time you begin to feel annoyed or frustrated by him, turn your focus to this list and instead of sending out negative thoughts about him send out positive ones. If you concentrate on these positively-geared affirmations you will soon find that you begin creating the workplace (or whatever else it is) that you desire.

It is important not to worry about the details of how the change will come to you. Instead of worrying about how you could possibly begin to feel differently about your job, just keep focusing on the positive things in your life and let the universe take care of the details. Remember that you are connected to everything that is, so when you focus your creative energy upon what you want, provided it is in a positive format, the whole universe will shift to give you what you desire. What you want is what it wants. You might find that your boss starts acting more nicely or even leaves the company. You may get promoted to a different department or find another job altogether, not to mention the possibility of winning the lottery and retiring, or having an epiphany and starting your own business...

The point is that humans cannot comprehend the diverse mechanisms at the disposal of the universe. Do not worry about the hows and whens of life, just make sure you are sending the right message out to the cosmos. If you stand back and let it unfold you will find yourself awed by the sheer brilliance of the universe's path to manifesting your most heartfelt desire.

Whilst acknowledging the importance of a positively-geared outlook on life, many of us simply do not manage to break away from mindsets that hold us back from achieving what we really want. All too often we choose to blame our situation on the people around us or the societies and systems in which we find ourselves. These complaints are not unreasonable. It can be very difficult to change our ways, especially after many years of reinforcement. Luckily for those of us who feel this way, there is an important key that can help us unlock these self-imposed shackles – that key of course being spiritual practice. By adopting a daily spiritual art designed to bring the body, mind and soul together, we will find negative tendencies and thought patterns much easier to leave behind us.

Remember that by doing your daily practice you are bringing the mind and body into synch with the soul, and the soul deeply desires to transcend the hurdles and difficulties of life as we know it. You will find the soul extending its influence over the mind and body, over your thoughts and actions, to bring you closer to the enlightenment it desires. You will thus transcend the attitudes and negative patterns that are holding back so many people today.

All is One

We live in a world of illusion, a world created to give impressions of things that do not exist. We live within this illusion so that we can experience ourselves, and through so doing, God can experience itself. Part of the ultimate experience of self is the realisation of the true self, the realisation of the illusion and the corresponding change in the way we live our lives.

That is why you are reading this book – so that you can see the true nature of the illusory world within which we live. So that you can see that although it often seems otherwise, we are not individual entities wading through a sea of foreignness, but are all connected and in fact one entity. So that you can see that we are not the physical beings we often presume ourselves to be, but energy beings existing within an unfathomably large field of energy. So that you can remember that life is not a string of events that happen to you, but rather a sequence of circumstances that you create through your thoughts, beliefs and the innermost desires of your soul.

There is another illusion which we must learn to see through. We generally view our world as a slowly-evolving concern that changes at a snail's pace through the ages. This need not be the case, as it is only through the tricks of time that we continue to create our world to look and act the way it does. Contrary to what we presume, our world is created afresh all the time, but the reason that we do not realise this is that it is re-created in the moment by thoughts and beliefs of the past. As such, our current thoughts and reactions will create our future to come. What we need to do in order to ensure the sort of future we desire is to stop reacting to the present in such a predictable fashion and begin reacting with our future realities in mind – begin reacting as unified beings guided by the desire of the soul.

The Spiritual Revolution

The evolution of humankind, as recorded in our history books, tells a tale of substantial growth and development. Over millennia, our societies have developed and changed from those of cave-dwelling people, completely preoccupied with survival, to the high-speed world of convenience and technology within which we live today. We have invested massive amounts of time and energy to arrive at the point that we are at now. As a result of this, we have created a world that is designed to cater for all of our physical needs and which replaces exertion with convenience.

Through the observation of our evolution, it becomes apparent that humankind has placed its focus most heavily on the physical aspects of our existence, relegating development of the mind to second place and investing comparatively little energy in further developing our spiritual selves. For instance, while most of us no longer invest time and energy in foraging and hunting for food, and receive more mental stimulation from our education system than in times gone by, we very often still support the same fear-based models of spirituality that were on offer thousands of years ago.

This focus on our physical surroundings is synonymous with the tendency we have to think of ourselves predominantly as physical beings. In fact, we often relate so much to the physical world that we somewhat ignore the spiritual side of life. While our physical bodies are of extreme importance, they only make up a third of the whole that is any one of us. Human beings are made up of three primary facets, three aspects of self that combine to form the whole that is you or me. One of these three facets is the physical self, which we have strived to cater for so thoroughly. Then there is the mental aspect which we have come to relate to so well through our constant search for information and knowledge. And finally, the spiritual facet of our being makes up the third part of the whole that is in each of us. Hence the birth of the New Age term, 'Body, Mind and Spirit'.

The extreme advancements that we have made in the effort to fulfil our physical and mental needs have left humanity in an exciting position. We have now, more than ever before, freed up our time and energy to explore the third aspect of our existence, the spiritual facet of our being. As a result of creating systems and mechanisms to cater for our physical and mental needs, we no longer need to expend our energy fulfilling these basic requirements and theoretically have more energy to explore other aspects of our selves. In other words, because we do not have to hunt and gather food, or live a nomadic lifestyle, we should be able to pour the energy previously used for basic survival into something else. We have, however, created ample distractions to captivate this newfound time and energy. Our consumer society provides us with abundant opportunities to become caught up in the materialistic aspects of life, and our multimedia systems provide more than enough mindless distraction to keep us from further exploring the realm of spirituality.

Nevertheless, I believe that the time of spiritual evolution is now upon us. It is my opinion that this is the underlying reason that we have created this situation of comparatively little basic need. We have sub-consciously engineered our current situation to make time and energy available to further explore the spiritual aspect of our being. In fact, I believe that we can see evidence of this shift towards a higher level of spirituality already taking place, simply by taking a walk through the ever growing Body, Mind, Spirit sections of our local bookstores. The interest in new ideas and interpretations of our spiritual significance is growing fast. There are more and more books like this one, appearing on the bookshelves all the time, and more and more conversations about our spirituality taking place than ever before. With this energy and willingness to explore our spirituality, we can begin to understand our place in the universe, and in so doing, learn to use our creative nature to the full extent of our potential. In a world where everything has meaning and there is no such thing as coincidence, the fact that we have freed up so much energy must be significant. It is my hope that we are now entering a period of spiritual awakening in which we will realise our connection to everything that surrounds us and by doing so, take a big step towards creating a world of enlightenment and bliss for all.

When looking at our world, it is easy to see a place of gloom, full of greed, fear and hatred. But if we take a step back and look at humankind's situation in relation to where we were a thousand or even a hundred years ago, it becomes evident that we are heading in the right direction. We are now entering a time of grand spiritual awakening that will bring with it the dawn of an era of peace and love, and the awakening of the knowledge that All is One.

....

In a world where nothing is coincidental and everything holds within it deeper purpose, our current situation is not one of chance. It is not the random degradation of society that some think it to be, but a vital position on the path to humankind's enlightenment. It is my belief that we are now entering into a period of immense spiritual evolution. We have already invested enough time and energy into the development of our physical selves and the furthering of our minds. Now is the time for our grand spiritual awakening, the renaissance of the spirit, where we can begin to live by the truth that we are connected to everything that surrounds us and that All is, in fact, One.

....

Part Two

All is One

The second part of this book is dedicated to transforming the philosophies of Part One into action for the realisation of peace, love, joy and harmony within our world. Part Two highlights areas of life that are in particular need of addressing and suggests ways in which we can go about bringing healing to these parts of our existence.

All the great sages, prophets and spiritual leaders who fill the pages of our history books had, at the very least, two things in common. The first of these is that each and every one of them was a thinker in the deepest sense of the word. Each of them was the embodiment of thought and questioning. All of these inspirational figures went beyond the realm of apathetic acceptance that envelops so many people today. They went beyond and dared to think about and question the deeper issues of life. It is from this questioning that they opened themselves up to receive the spiritual inspiration for which they are so famous.

Stories from the lives of Buddha, Jesus and Muhammad illustrate this well. Gautama Siddhartha, the father of Buddhism, was born the son of a king. He grew up living a sheltered and lavish life full of the earthly luxuries of which most people dream. Yet despite his sheltered lifestyle, questions arose within him. He could not help noticing the suffering in the lives of the servants around him, their sadness, illness and death. His observations drove him to leave his life of luxury and go in search of the solutions to the despair of humankind. His need for answers about our existence was so strong that he left his palace and lived in the woods where he spent years meditating and fasting before his enlightenment underneath the bodhi tree.

Tales from the gospel of Luke tell of Jesus at the age of twelve spending three days in discussion with Jewish teachers in a temple in Jerusalem, listening and asking questions that astounded all who were present, questions that led to his enlightenment after meeting John the Baptist.

Stories of Muhammad tell of a man who would spend several weeks every year meditating in a cave in the mountains surrounding Mecca. At the age of forty, Muhammad, feeling discontented with life, retreated to his cave for a time of meditation and reflection.

It was at this moment that Allah first appeared to him.

Spiritual insight and inspiration is naturally not reserved for sages alone. We too can access this sort of knowledge. Spiritual insight is revealed to any mind that asks. By asking the right questions about our existence, we create space for the answers to flow to us. Without questioning, there cannot be space for answers. Therefore the inspiration cannot flow to the mind that does not call to it. The drive to question and the tenacity to think freely work as the foundations upon which all meaningful spiritual realisations are built.

The habit of questioning and the tendency towards free thinking are not all the sages like Mohammed, Jesus, and Gautama Buddha have in common. Each of these figures took their spiritual insight to the next level, the level of action. There are many among us who have become adept at the art of questioning but have not yet taken their answers to the level where they are able to grow from thought into action. Inspired thought is not enough to fulfil a being living in a world of movement and action like our own. In order to find the fulfilment and enlightenment for which our souls long, we need to learn to express our spiritual inspiration through our actions in the same way that the spiritual masters who came before us have done.

The Staircase of Human Identities

In Part One, I spoke about how we live our lives by the illusory perception of separation. We tend to think that we are separate from everything that surrounds us, even though in our most basic state, we are connected to absolutely everything that exists. Although we perceive ourselves primarily as individual physical beings, the inescapable truth is that our physicality is only the perception of energy vibrating at different speeds. Although we see ourselves as physical beings living within a physical world, we are actually pockets of energy living and interacting within a world of energy. We are not the individual entities we see ourselves as; we are essentially expressions of the divine energy who have forgotten our true identity for the sake of experiencing individuality.

In a universe where everything is connected to everything else, where all that we perceive as separate and individual is in fact one, there cannot exist lack and scarcity. There is always enough to fulfil each and every need. There is always enough to gratify any desire that could ever be felt. Whenever any aspect of the universe feels a desire or experiences a need, the entire cosmos shifts to create that which will fulfil the desire and assuage the need. A single entity that has the omnipotent ability to create anything could not act in any other way, for to do so it would willingly deny itself what it desires. Sadly we live out our lives blinded to this truth. We do not realise that we are intimately connected to everything that is, and as a result of this we do not realise that the universe would gladly give us everything we desire. Instead we have cultivated the belief that only limited resources exist with which to fulfil our needs. As always, our thoughts and beliefs are the seeds from which our experiences sprout. Our belief that a limited amount of resources exist creates the illusion that suggests lack and scarcity to be the truth.

The belief that there is not enough to go around and that someone will therefore have to go without, gives rise to an infectious fear-based mentality that drives us to believe even more strongly that we are separate from those around us. Through the belief that somebody will have to go without is born the fear that this somebody could turn out to be me. This fear then gives rise to a feeling of panic, which we use to justify actions of greed and selfishness. Because we are worried that there are limited universal resources available to us, we tend to try to grab as much as we can as fast as we can, and greedily guard it from those who we perceive as separate from ourselves.

I have been privileged in my life to grow up surrounded by artists. Sculptors, painters and potters have always been as much a part of the scenery as birds, trees and grass. Within the art world I have been able to notice a clear divide between successful artists and the numerous unsuccessful ones. It seemed to me that the success of an artist has only a small amount to do with his or her talent. In fact I would go so far as to say that the most talented artist I have ever come across is still, after many years of creating the most amazing pieces, battling to make ends meet. The reason for this is that he, like many others, believes the world to be a place of lack, a place where there is only a finite amount of money and praise on offer and that we all need to fight for it. I remember another artist I knew a few years ago who, despite being mediocre in his talent, was a charismatic character who seemed to always presume that his work would sell and that there simply was plenty of money, success and affluence to spread his way. So of course this was the experience he had and his pieces flew out of the galleries like hot cakes. The only thing that separated these two artists is that one believed that there was plenty to go around and the other supported the fear-based mentality of lack in which so many people are currently trapped.

Although we predominantly perceive ourselves to be individual physical beings, we have not restricted ourselves to this single classification of identity. We have created an entire hierarchy of identities and non-identities, which we use to classify what we both belong to and are separate from. We swap and change between these different identities due to the situations within which we find ourselves and choose how to act in accordance with each particular circumstance. The different groups with which we identify determine with whom we share our resources and against whom we guard them. I liken this multi-faceted system of identity and non-identity to a six-stepped staircase. Each step represents a different level of identification, thus determining with whom we do and do not identify at the time and therefore, whom we do and do not see as a threat to our limited resources. The size and sort of group with which we identify varies as one climbs up the metaphorical staircase and ranges from a singular identification with the physical body on the first step to a complete universal identification on the sixth.

It is important to remember that we swap and change between these different forms of identity all the time. One moment we may find ourselves glimpsing sixth step enlightenment and the next be caught up with the perception of lack on a different tier altogether. Therefore the staircase is not a progression that we follow, but rather something that we hop up and down on, in a seemingly higgledy-piggledy fashion.

Step One:

On the first step of the staircase we perceive ourselves purely as individuals adrift in a sea of foreignness. As a result, we perceive everything from a 'me or them' perspective and do not relate to any group at all. From this perspective we even view our family members as separate from ourselves. Children often display this sort of behaviour. Picture a small boy stuffing himself with chocolate cake until he cannot eat any more. Then he sees his sister come around the corner and he quickly squashes the last slice into his chocolate-smeared mouth so that she cannot get it.

One of the prime currencies of this first step is none other than money. There is a flawed perception that there is not enough wealth to spread around for all of us. From this idea of lack is created the poisonous mentality of greed. Many of us spend our whole lives trying to amass as much money as we possibly can, missing out on life so that we can die with as many zeros in our bank accounts as possible.

Life is for living, love is for loving and money is for spending. There is enough wealth in the world for each and every one of us to live the lives we want to be living right now. Our greedy mentality that tells us that there is a shortage of wealth drives us to hoard money for later in life when there are others that need it now. The truth is that if we all kept our money cycling through our lives, there would be enough wealth for everyone.

We have to remember that not everyone wants to be the next Richard Branson or the Queen of England. Certainly, if that were the case, then the wealth in the world would not stretch far enough to service us all. But everyone is wonderfully unique and we all want different experiences from life. The accountant and the monk from Part One find their happiness in different places and accordingly need different amounts of wealth to live out their lives. As long as we each pursue that which really makes us happy, and not just what our society tells us we should pursue, there will be precisely enough wealth in the world for us all.

The problem that trips up the system is that the wealthy echelons of society are storing up riches in bulging bank accounts due to fear of it somehow running out. We need to learn to trust that our wealth will return to us – and keep it moving. Money is a representation of energy and energy must flow. If we all let our wealth cycle through our lives, we would find that we would all always have enough of what we need when we need it.

Remember that your thoughts and attitudes create your future. If you cycle your wealth and keep it flowing, you are sending out a message that says you are wealthy and consequently more wealth will come your way. But if you scrimp and save too much, believing there to be a shortage of wealth on offer, then a shortage is what you will experience.

While we were in Taiwan, a Taiwanese friend translated a newspaper article for me. In Taiwan every transaction made to and from a bank account is printed out in a small booklet that is updated each time a visit is made to the bank, with the grand total neatly underlined on the bottom of the page. The newspaper article was about a wealthy man who had died a couple of days earlier. The story described how, when the body of the man was found, he was lying on his back with his bankbook clutched to his chest. What good did the stockpile of wealth do this man on his deathbed? The answer of course is absolutely none.

There is no need for greed as there is always enough to go around. Money is worthless unless we let it cycle and if we do it will always come back to us. We should hope that we do not end up like the Taiwanese man, clinging to his first step identification and addiction to the fictitious numbers on the bottom line of his booklet. Remember that generosity creates more with which to be generous. Only when we learn to give freely, will we be able to fully experience the magnitude of our wealth. This was re-affirmed to me some years ago when my wife and I returned home from 18 months living abroad. In that time we had managed to acquire all the appliances and other odds and ends of a comfortable lifestyle. Instead of trying to sell our belongings, we decided to give everything away to our friends, so we had a party and sent everyone home with gifts in their arms. A couple of weeks later, when we were back in South Africa, our generosity was returned to us many times over. We were out in the countryside, visiting friends when we found out that they had just decided to emigrate. They asked us if we would be interested in moving into the farmhouse where they had been staying and taking care of the farm for a while. Excitedly we agreed and told all of our friends and family about our new plan. By the time we moved onto the farm we had the pick of three complete households of furniture and appliances that 'by chance' were offered to us. So it was that from having nothing, we moved into our fully-furnished home without spending a cent.

Recently I was fortunate enough to attend an incredible talk given by the famous Buddhist, Geshe Michael Roach. The Geshe spoke about the power of giving and that it is the nature of the universe to return our gifts to us many times over. The Geshe likened giving to those in need, and other similar acts of compassion, to that of the planting of seeds within the mind. He said that when we give to those in need, to good people who we believe are truly in need of what we are giving, it is like planting a seed in rich fertile soil. Seeds planted in good soil will grow strong and bear much fruit – the fruit being the returning of our generosity in our time of need. Conversely, he said that should we plant our seeds in bad soil, in a place in which we do not believe or see a proper need, then the plants will wither and die before they can bear fruit. The Geshe also spoke about how the art of giving can and does inspire others to give, especially when they see the bountiful fruit grown from the seeds of compassion. He closed by saying that should we intend that the fruits of our giving travel beyond us, then the act of giving becomes even more powerful.

Step Two:

On the second step of the staircase, we no longer identify with ourselves alone. Here we see our families and other very close-knit groups as connected to ourselves, while those that do not fall within these intimate groups continue to be viewed as separate. As a result of this we allow ourselves to ignore the immediate needs of others whilst justifying actions that provide for needs that our family may one day have. How often do we find a situation where people stash away vast stockpiles of wealth for future use by their families, while others are starving to death? Because we think that there is a scarcity of good things out there, we store them away for the future and, as a result, do others out of the means to obtain the basic needs of life. In almost every city in the world we can find numerous wealthy families amassing fortunes that far surpass their needs, whilst within a matter of kilometres there are other families that do not have roofs over their heads or food in their stomachs. Of course this does not mean that we should not take care of those close to us or that we should never prepare for our children's futures. It is always good to ask ourselves if we would still make the same decisions if we knew that there would always be enough for what we want to do when we need it. If our answer is yes, then we know we are on the right track. If not, we may well find that the decisions we make were born through the illusion of lack and that they do not truly serve us.

This second step mentality of lack allows us to stand by and watch as orphaned children roam the streets of our world without food, shelter, parents or love. Because these children do not fall within our second step classification of family, we ignore their silent cries whilst spoiling our own children with everything they have ever wanted.

Every year the USA spends between two and three billion dollars on fertility treatment. This goes on year after year while children all over the world live on the streets without homes or families to care for them. The United Nations estimates that there are 150 million street children in the world today and that number is growing all the time. How can we spend so much money trying to have our 'own' children when there are so many already out there needing our support? The answer to this is that we are so preoccupied with this second step of identification that we do not care for the plight of these children as they fall outside of our second step 'us' group.

I was having a conversation with a friend of mine a little while ago and he told me a story that illustrates this sort of thinking very clearly. My friend's wife was pregnant with their first child at the time. They had just been to visit their family and told the grandfather-to-be about their plans to adopt a brother or sister in a few years rather than having a second child 'of their own'. This news deeply upset my friend's father. He thought that adopting a child would somehow betray the family and urged my friend to re-consider. This man was exhibiting classic second step identification. He was so caught up identifying with this insular family that he could not see the beauty and generosity of his son's decision, a decision that reaches beyond the confines of the second tier 'us' group to the world at large.

Can you imagine a world where those with excess give to those who needed instead of keeping what they do not need for those close to them alone? Can you imagine a world where every child is educated, clothed, loved and cared for? If you can imagine a world like this, then we are on the right track, as the seed has been planted.

If we can imagine this world, then in time we will be able to create it. The more of us who keep this picture of the world in our minds' eye, the more creative energy is released into our collective consciousness and the closer we get to creating this as a reality for all.

Step Three:

Stepping up once more, we find ourselves identifying with a multitude of different groups, whose boundaries extend beyond family and close friends. On this third step of self-classification we identify with others due to attributes, interests and beliefs shared in the fields of religion, political views, ethnic background, geographical proximity, gender, wealth and sexual preference.

On this step, just as we do on most of the others, we allow our feelings of separation to justify committing all manner of atrocities against those who we perceive as separate from ourselves – and therefore threatening to consume the resources we desire. Evidence of this behaviour is visible throughout humankind's history.

Slavery is a prime example of this third step behaviour. In times gone by, the so-called civilised societies of our globe thought little of violently tearing apart husband and wife, mother and child as they stole people's lives for convenience and monetary gain. The average wealthy person of that time thought little of enslaving other human beings, as long as they fell within a different ethnic or racial group. Simple differences of skin colour or origin were enough to justify behaviour that would otherwise have been deemed appalling.

Mass slaughter in the form of genocide is another illustration of this third step mentality that mars the pages of our history books. The Holocaust is a particularly sad example. During the Second World War, Nazi Germany killed an estimated six million Jewish men, women and children. The German authorities were able to condone this large-scale act of violence, because in their minds, they saw Jews as separate from themselves. Due to their ethnic background, the Jews were seen as a threat to the resources that Nazi Germany wanted to keep for itself alone.

Another example of third step brutality from the recent past, comes in the form of the Apartheid system that was in place in my home country of South Africa from 1948 to 1994. Here a small white minority segregated an entire country's population according to the colour of their skin, and purposefully oppressed all those whose skin colours were darker than their own. They did this for fear that the 'them' group might rise up and snatch the power that the government of the time so desired to keep. Ordinary people were able to justify atrocious treatment of their own countrymen for fear that if they did not, there would not be enough to go around to support both 'them' and the perceived 'us' group of the time.

Sadly, these examples of third step justification of inhumane behaviour are not only found in our history books, but continue to flourish in our modern day world. The ceaseless unrest and violence in the Gaza and West Bank areas of the Middle East serve to illustrate this well. Here, the Israelis and Palestinians continue fighting, after more than sixty years of conflict as a result of differences in the religious beliefs of their forefathers.

The disheartening truth is that this sort of behaviour will continue to haunt humankind's future until we recognise the illusory nature of our perception of lack and begin to live by the reality that All is One. We must realise that we are connected to everyone around us, regardless of skin colour, gender, sexual preference or religious views.

Step Four:

With the next step up the staircase, our sense of belonging and non-belonging broadens to a national identity. On this fourth step we use the countries in which we live to distinguish between who is a part of the 'us' group and who is relegated to 'them'. Looking at the world map on the wall in front of me, I see an irregular patchwork of many shapes and colours. Each of these small patches is connected to all of those that border it, yet each of them is very definitely confined and separated by an unmistakable barrier that lies between it and the piece against which it so snugly fits. We have taken the globe upon which we live and systematically divided it up into little pieces that we consider to be separate to those around them, even though there is often no physical divide or difference between one portion of land and the next. This systematic dissection of our Earth's surface is indicative of the mentality of this fourth step of classification. Here we apply a sort of sliding scale of morality to determine what is acceptable behaviour towards those who live within our national circle, while at the same time creating a different set of standards for those living outside this boundary. This is the home of nationalism and patriotism. From here we view all other countries but our own as a threat to our prosperity. We justify committing heinous crimes against entire nations in an attempt to protect what we see as ours, or even try to take that which we want that belongs to 'them'. We hurriedly stash away as much as we can get our hands on and greedily withhold it from other nations in their times of need.

A look at the International Monetary Fund's (IMF) depiction of the various Gross Domestic Products (GDP) of the world's nations for for 2010[2], illustrates this point well. This is a list of the world's countries and the total value of all of the final goods and services produced by each country within a year. The IMF estimated that there existed a grand total of over USD $62,000,000 million of wealth on the globe in 2010. Of this, the USA alone possessed well over USD $14,000,000 million. This equates to the USA possessing over 23% of the world's gross wealth. What this means is that, at that time, a country that has less than 5% of the world's population held almost a quarter of the world's wealth. Compare this to India, the second largest national population behind China. India accounts for approximately 17% of the global population, yet it only possesses a little over 2% of the global wealth.

To illustrate this inequality more clearly one can look at the Gross Domestic Product (GDP) in terms of what this amount would mean to the individuals of a country, were it equally divided up amongst them. Of course this does not actually happen and the truth is that within each nation the wealth is unevenly divided. This calculation serves to illustrate the wealth of our countries in relation to their populations. For 2010 the IMF estimated the GDP per capita (per person) of the USA at over USD $47,000 and that of Zimbabwe at USD $594. What this means is that the average person in the USA would have earned more within four days than the average Zimbabwean would have earned over the entire year. As I write (2011), Zimbabwe's situation has deteriorated even further. Zimbabwe currently houses hundreds of thousands of people who are starving within a country that has an unemployment rate of over 95%[3]. Zimbabwe has hit financial ruin. Yet few other countries seem to be coming to its aid. As nations, we sit by and watch as others starve and die, when we have much more wealth than we need.

In the world right now less that 5% of the population holds over 23% of the wealth. Millions starve because they do not have the means to purchase their next meal. Would a world where this inequality could be forgotten not be a fantastic place? Imagine a world where our wealthy countries gave to the needy without fearing for the future, as they knew that should they be in the same situation, others with excess would gladly give to them.

Step Five:

The fifth step of the staircase is where our sense of identity grows from a national level to a unity with all humankind. On this step we identify with humankind as a whole, but exclude all that is not a part of the human race. Here, the 'us' is all of humankind and the 'them' is the rest of the non-human world. On this level of identity we are able to justify almost any action that is seen to benefit humankind, with little or no consideration of how it affects the rest of our globe.

On this step, unlike those that preceded it, we are not driven by the fear of 'them' consuming the resources we see before us. The reason for this is that humankind as a whole tends to see that which is non-human as inferior. We generally seem to be of the opinion that we are special because we possess consciousness. We mistakenly presume that the non-human 'them' does not possess the life force that we recognise within human beings. We fail to recognise this same life force within our surroundings because we seldom stop long enough to look at the splendour of our natural world. What this ultimately means is that we do not see the non-human world as a threat to humankind and therefore we are not driven out of fear to attack 'it' before 'it' gets 'us'. This is not to say that we do not abuse the perceived 'them' circle. In fact, due to our inability to identify with the non-human 'them', the non-humankind often suffers the brunt of our mistreatment. Our Earth and everything that lives and grows upon her is under constant bombardment as a result of our haste to grab at the resources we see before us. It is the sad truth that the great majority of humankind battles to transcend this hurdle of consciousness. As a result, we tend to think little of the impact that our actions have on the natural world that sustains us. The ever-increasing growth in annual extinctions of non-human species depicts this disregard well.

Extinctions are something totally natural on our globe. Throughout the Earth's history many species have become extinct in a perfectly balanced and natural way. Our world evolves and the species that cannot evolve with global change become extinct. However, the extreme rate at which this is now happening is not natural. Humankind's negative impact upon the globe is having a huge effect on all those with whom we share her and due to this, a hugely disproportionate amount of species are becoming extinct or are currently under threat of extinction. In fact, it has been estimated by the International Union for Conservation of Nature (IUCN)[4] that the current extinction rate is between 1,000 to 10,000 times that which it should naturally be. Humankind disassociates from the non-human world to the degree that we can justify a way of life that is driving between 1,000 to 10,000 times more species into extinction than would naturally occur if it were not for our abusive behaviour.

In their 2008 Red List, the IUCN calculated that of the 5,487 recorded species of land mammals, 1,141 are currently threatened (that is to say, critically endangered, endangered or vulnerable). This means that one in five of every mammalian species that we know of, is considered endangered.

As for species of birds, 1,226 of the 9,856 listed species are considered threatened – that is more than 12% of all known species.

In terms of plant life, Dycotyledons (non-grass flowering plants) which are seldom used for commercial purposes, have been hit particularly hard – 74% of these plants are currently under threat of premature extinction.

The sad truth is that, because of our acute inability to identify with the non-human world, be it the world of birds, bees, trees or ocean creatures, we are abusing our natural surroundings in a way that is utterly shameful. We need to remember that the environment that surrounds us and the animals that live within it are equally important to ourselves. They too are God Energy living out an expression of divinity.

The good news, however, is that although the current situation may be dismal, we do not need to continue down this gloomy path. If we begin to live by the philosophy that All is One and transcend this fifth step mentality, we would have no option but to cherish the natural world that surrounds us and restore it to a state of harmony and balance.

Disease and the Fifth Step

In nature all species of plants and animals balance each other out to create and maintain a state of environmental harmony. If the population of antelope in the plains of Africa grows to an unsustainable size, the grasslands will not be able to provide adequate grazing and the population will die down until, once again, there is enough grass to sustain the herd. In addition, should there be a swelling in the herds of antelope, their natural predators will thrive and in so doing, begin to predate more heavily upon the antelope until their population is again reduced. Conversely, should the predators overpopulate a particular area, they will consume their food source, the antelope, to the point where there are not enough left to sustain the size of their packs or prides. The older and weaker predators will die off until a sustainable balance is once again reached.

All species found within our atmosphere, except one, complement each other in this way. Humankind has evolved beyond its natural predators and in doing so has broken its harmonious relationship with all that surrounds it. We have broken away from the natural management of our population and have only ourselves left to control the size and health of our species. Sadly though, we have not yet come up with a harmonious manner in which to do this and we all too often subconsciously resort to war, genocide and disease to keep ourselves in check.

Seth Falconer

It is easy for anyone to see how war and genocide are human-created occurrences, but many of us fail to realise that the diseases that threaten our existence are something for which we are wholly responsible. We create our realities and on a collective level we create the diseases we experience within them.

Because we no longer live in symbiosis with nature, we have created sickness to help keep our population in balance. And so, until humankind realises its responsibility towards the Earth and learns to balance itself in a peaceful and healthy way, we will be destined to live in a world of epidemic and disease. It is the responsibility of each and every one of us to consider the strain that our global population and way of life is putting on the Earth and to make decisions in a manner that works toward easing the load we put on the environment. Among other detrimental habits, the growth of our population through oversized families needs to be addressed. The days of having many children should have passed. There are already enough children wandering the streets of our world without each couple bringing two or three more into the picture. It is time for a birth of compassion towards both the Earth and our fellow people. If we want a house full of happy little voices, fill it with those who are already here.

This is not to say that we need deny ourselves the beautiful experience of creating and giving birth to a child. We should do it once, but then look to the need in the world and fill the gaps in our existence with the tiny hearts pleading to be loved.

When we all get serious about the management of our population, we will find that there will no longer be any need for disease and we will be able to begin living lives free of the pain and suffering that come as part of our current package. Before we can do this we need to become aware of the process we use to create sickness and disease.

Sickness on a Personal Level

Humankind's recent fascination with how things work, instead of why they do, has led to an extreme imbalance in our perception of sickness and disease. Our scientific preoccupation with understanding how our bodies function has given birth to an unwholesome approach to our health. When we get sick, we tend to fall back on the popular trend of treating the symptoms of our ailment with a clever cocktail of chemicals, without ever stopping to consider why we got sick in the first place. As we already know, everything that we experience is the direct manifestation of energy from the realm of thought, intermingled with our soul's deepest desires. It should not surprise us that our sicknesses and ailments are no exception. When our mind is in a state of harmony, our body follows suit with a state of perfect health. Conversely, when we lose the balance within our mind, we will physically express our inner imbalance through a lapse in our outer health.

I have noticed a direct parallel between my outer body and my inner mind through the practice or non-practice of a spiritual art. I have found that to maintain a healthy and peaceful inner sanctum I need to frequently engage in meditative activities. This for me usually takes the shape of my daily yoga practice but can also be through sitting cross-legged and meditating, sitting silently by a flowing river or even writing in my journal. Without fail, if I go for a few days without setting aside time for my meditation, I begin to notice my mind clouding over with noise and bustle. At this point I should recognise my need for introspection, but sometimes do not. In these instances I invariably begin to feel run down, my body gets tired quickly, my back gets stiff, my head begins to hurt. These are all symptoms physically expressed to alert me to the fact that the peace within my mind has been disrupted. Thankfully, at this point I generally cotton on to the imbalance. If I don't I am sure that my body would begin to express the inner imbalance more forcefully, which could ultimately lead to the manifestation of sickness and disease.

Many Eastern spiritual and health practices use the chakra system to connect imbalances in the mental realm with their physical repercussions. Each chakra or energy centre within our bodies pertains to both a physical area of the body and an aspect of our mental and spiritual selves. When we feel a physical sickness or ailment, we are able, through the use of the chakra system, to track the problem back to the area of our thinking and attitudes from which it came. For example, should I experience a sore throat, I would be experiencing an imbalance in the throat chakra. As a result of this, I could deduce that I may be experiencing a sore throat because of an inability to clearly express my thoughts and desires. This knowledge would give me the opportunity to work out what it is that I am struggling to express and provide me with the opportunity to restore balance to my inner sanctum. In so doing, I would be able to heal the root cause of my ailment.

Unfortunately, the majority of us tend to buy into the Western paradigm that suggests our health is a purely physical affair. In doing this, we give over the responsibility of our health to physicians and doctors, when in truth we are each the masters of our own well-being and the only ones responsible for it. This surrender of responsibility brings about further trouble for the individual. As we know, what we believe governs the nature of our experiences. When we believe our health to be a precarious concern over which we have little control, this becomes our future experience. If we think that people get sick at random, then we open ourselves up to all sorts of sickness and disease. If we believe that we are at risk of getting cancer because 'so many people fall prey to this terrible disease', then we are likely to. Of course, the opposite is also true. If we take responsibility for our health and listen to what our bodies tell us, taking into account the root causes of our physical ailments, then we would have no reason to live in fear of contracting random sicknesses. This is not to say that we will never get sick again. But we can be sure that whatever ailments we encounter are either the result of a personal imbalance or purposeful creation of the soul for a deeper purpose, not a fear-based attitude of society.

Sickness and Disease on a Global Level

Just as imbalances in our personal minds create their physical counterparts, so too do imbalances within our collective mind create collective physical repercussions. In the same way that different energy centres throughout our bodies are linked to different aspects of our minds, different diseases represent specific imbalances within our collective mind. Take HIV for example. HIV/AIDS is a sexually transmitted disease, which was accountable for two million deaths in 2007. The fact that this is a sexually-transmitted disease would, on an individual level, indicate problems with the base chakra, which governs, amongst other things, sexuality. What this means on a global scale is that HIV/AIDS is created as a result of a massive imbalance regarding sexuality within our collective mind. For the last two millennia the Western world has been governed by organisations that teach that sex is a bad and sinful thing. This sort of large-scale negativity passed down through centuries has created massive amounts of negative energy surrounding sex. As a result we have created this horrific sexually-transmitted disease.

The truth is, as long as it is shared between consenting adults, there is absolutely nothing wrong with sex. When used in the right context, sex is one of the most fantastic expressions of love that we are physically capable of. But in order for us to be able to transcend HIV/AIDS and all other sexually-transmitted diseases, we need to first take responsibility for ourselves as a species and begin living in harmony with our Earth. Then we need to shift our thinking about sex from being a negative sinful thing to being a wonderful exploration of love and affection. By doing so, the positive energy surrounding sex will be able to displace the old negativity, and sex will once again become a wondrous thing to be explored with joy.

When we take responsibility for our species, there will no longer be any need to kill ourselves off with sickness, violence and disease. When we take responsibility for our health as individuals, we will no longer need to live in fear of plagues, epidemics and viruses. Then humankind will at last be able to live in harmony with all that surrounds us.

Step Six:

On the sixth and last step of the staircase we identify on a universal level. We no longer distinguish between what we perceive as physically separate from ourselves in our everyday lives, but realise our connection to everything that is. This is where we experience the all-knowing perception of total unity, where we realise the illusory nature of all the various forms of identity by which we live our lives. On this level of identity we learn to transcend the illusions of separation and the mentality of 'us and them'. We lose the sliding scale of morality that allows us to commit the atrocities we readily commit on the other steps of the metaphorical staircase. Here we experience what the Buddhist faith calls enlightenment; we know our total unity with everything and can begin to live in a world of peace, love and harmony. When humankind's collective soul reaches this level of identification and learns to use it as the foundation from which we live out our lives, there will be no option but to restore everything before us to a state of harmonious perfection. When we realise that All is One, we will no longer be able to justify abusive actions towards others because we fear what they say or want what they have, as this fear will no longer find sanctuary within our hearts.

When we no longer see the beggar on the street as separate from ourselves, we will no longer hold back the excess we have from the needy. When we no longer see children as someone else's and not our own, we will no longer let any small stomachs go hungry or any young hearts go unloved. When we no longer distinguish between 'us' and 'them' as a result of race, religion and sexuality, then we will no longer wish to enslave, abuse and kill. When we begin to see Americans, Africans, Europeans and Asians as extensions of ourselves, we will no longer be able to wage war on another society because we want what 'they' have, or fear what 'they' say. When we no longer see our surroundings as resources waiting to be abused, and realise that we are One with everything, then we will begin to live in a world of balance, harmony and peace. When we no longer consider ourselves to be separate and learn to live our lives as One, we will begin to experience the bliss that life is meant to be.

Like chameleons changing colour to suit their surroundings, we swap and change our sense of identity to make ourselves fit the circumstances in which we find ourselves. One moment we may see ourselves as individuals struggling to keep our heads afloat against the tide, and the next see ourselves as part of a family, team or nation.

The reality is that no matter how real these identities may seem, there is only one true identity, the universal identity that comes with the realisation that All is One. We are each a part of a single glorious whole and that whole is God. The key to our happiness and that of everyone that surrounds us lies in this realisation. When we each learn to live our lives from this enlightened perspective, our Earth will begin to dance with the ecstasy of perfect harmony.

Education

When we are born, we are like lumps of clay waiting to be transformed into beautiful works of art. The raw clay holds within it the potential to become absolutely anything and go anywhere. The potter's hands then guide this limitless potential, and through gentle persuasion, transform it into a fixed shape, only one of the countless forms that the clay could become. In this way, the potential of the clay is tethered to the limitations placed upon it by the potter's hands.

When we are born, we are the lumps of clay, bursting with potential to do absolutely anything and become absolutely anyone. Right from day one, the potters of our lives begin the ongoing process of manipulating our potential in this way or that and without knowing it, they begin conditioning our limitless nature into a form that teaches us to believe ourselves to be so much less than we truly are.

We all have numerous potters throughout the duration of our lives, people who form the way we think and how we see the world. The first artists of our lives are usually our parents and the other members of our immediate families. Right from when we are born, we look to those around us for examples of how to deal with the world. We watch them to get ideas of how we should expect the world around us to behave and how we should in turn react to it. We gradually adopt their picture of how things are, along with the limitations they perceive as governing their lives. Then, as we get older our social circle begins to increase. For most of us, this occurs when we first go to school. At this point, we acquire a new group of potters to help mould us day by day. Our school teachers are the ones responsible for the formal side of our education, and accordingly, it is from them that we learn with more detail how our surroundings are believed to work. It is in our schools that we are quietly programmed with whatever the popular paradigm of our current society happens to be. Like sponges thirsty for information, we absorb the limitations we are taught to believe without question.

While a formal education is certainly a positive thing for any young mind, it can, if not properly administered, also be detrimental to the remainder of the individual's life. As we have already explored, what we believe inevitably becomes the truth of our realities. Our beliefs create our realities, and so, if we are taught to believe in false limitations, these will inevitably become the boundaries within which our realities will exist. If we are taught to believe ourselves to be less than we truly are, then these beliefs will become the truths of our lives.

Most of us go through our childhood and teenage years quietly accepting what we are told about the world. We take in the paradigm of human existence that our families and teachers believe without questioning. We believe the picture portrayed by them, because it is the only one to which we have had access. It is often only when we break away from the artists of our early lives that we come across the opportunity to re-think the way we view our place in the world. When we fly from the metaphorical nest and leave our childhood homes, we come across the chance to question the concepts passed down to us by our various potters and should we choose to, we can begin creating our own new vision of the world. Sadly though, many of us never quite manage to break away from the negative aspects of our childhood potters and as a result, their limiting views of the world live on through our lives.

If we were taught to see things differently from a young age, if our potters moulded us into beings that realise our true potential, then we could bypass the limitations that the previous generations experienced and take a leap forward in the spiritual evolution of humankind. Remember the game I used to play with my Taiwanese class? Imagine if the 'telepathic' abilities of my class were trained and honed throughout their entire schooling. Would this not be a fantastic tool to prepare these children for the rest of their lives? Young children are waiting to learn about the mysteries of our world, so why not start teaching them.

What we should be looking to do in order to initiate a spiritual leap forward, is to adapt our education systems to suit the needs of the time. Humankind is now at a point where we either need to learn to love our surroundings as we love ourselves, or we will exterminate all around us, and inevitably ourselves too. We are at the point where a spiritual evolution is becoming a necessity not a fancy. What better place to start the change than in the minds and hearts of the next generation? We already have schooling systems established in every corner of the globe. The next generation of children is already sitting in front of teachers, learning about the world and what we know about it. All we have to do is pay more attention to what we are teaching them.

Imagine a situation where children were trained to realise the God within themselves. Imagine a situation where, as well as learning addition, subtraction and division, our children are being taught to utilise the full extent of their limitless creative nature, and to understand and feel their connection to everything else. We need to develop the curricula of our schools into something that caters for all aspects of the human existence, not solely the physical. We should be coaching the young minds of our future to be able to see everything from a perspective of total unity, as well as from their individual perspective. We ought to teach our children the tools they need to leap over the spiritual hurdles that have tripped up the generations before them. What better place to do this than in our schools?

Of course our schools and their teachers are not the only potters who should re-evaluate their roles. Each and every one of us influences those around us, just as the artist manipulates the clay. We are all responsible for sculpting the new generation, as well as the maintenance of the present one. Consequently, we must ensure that the way we influence those around us is as positive as possible.

All is One

We must make sure that our actions encourage those around us to realise their infinite potential, not hold them back from it. We must be the sort of potter who inspires the clay to take on its own form of choice, free from restrictions, to achieve its most divine potential.

The best way to do this is to lead by good example. By living from the truth that All is One we not only create role models for others to follow, but also increase the thought energy relating to living a highly spiritual life. This makes it easier for others to make the change to an enlightened lifestyle. Of course as far as being potters goes, parenting is the most prominent area in which we affect the beliefs and understanding of the next generation. As parents, we have the unique opportunity to teach our children about their unity with everything as well as their creative role within our world, before the rest of society suggests otherwise. The wonderful thing about children is the flexibility of their imaginations. To a child the idea that he or she is a part of God, and that he or she is intimately connected to everything, is as easily acceptable as the idea that storks bring babies and that Father Christmas slides down chimneys to bring presents. So why not give children a spiritual head start and raise them to see their godly nature? Due to the growing strength of the spiritual revolution there are more and more storybooks appearing on the shelves designed to encourage our children to see things from this spiritual perspective right from the beginning. These books help to create a wonderful foundation upon which we can build through constant communication with our little ones, to raise them to transcend the hiccups of the previous generations.

We should never be afraid to show the marvels and gems that we have uncovered to those around us. Whether it be with the old or young, we can share our spiritual truth, as in doing so we bring change closer to becoming a reality.

Though you may not realise it, you are an artist of the highest degree. You are a potter of the finest material. Your medium is not earth and mud. You are an artist of potential.

It is important to know that with your artistic flare comes a deep responsibility towards your masterpieces. As you sculpt and form your artworks (the lives and minds of those around you) you set form to their previously limitless potential. Through what you do and the way that you do it, you create an example that the next generation eagerly mimics as they look for identity in a confusing world. In this way you pass your shortfalls on to the next generation. You teach them that they are less than they truly are. You need to stop this self-perpetuating cycle and begin teaching your children of their true potential, their Godly nature. Herein lies the key to the healing of our Earth and all to which you are connected.

Global Consciousness

The Earth is not dying, it is being killed, and those that are killing it have names and addresses.
Utah Philips

The sad truth is that humankind is steadily killing the Earth. The lifestyles that most of us lead have a hugely negative impact on the globe and all those with which we share her. Unfortunately the vast majority of us are unable to identify with our Earth and all others living upon her. We are all too often consumed by the illusion of separation, the mirage that disconnects us from our globe. The time has come for us to see through this illusion and realise our unity with the Earth that sustains us, to begin living by the truth that All is One. We need to become aware that almost all of our actions, whether going to work in the morning or buying a sandwich from the corner café, have a polluting effect on our Earth. The good news however, is that by making a few small changes to the way we live and becoming globally conscious, we can begin to live lives far more in line with harmony, peace and balance.

What it means to become globally conscious is to increase our awareness about the consequences of the small actions of our lives and to begin making sustainable choices. We all need to become aware that absolutely everything we do has consequences and that the Earth and all those living on her are paying the price for our lives of convenience and ignorance. Thankfully, many of us have already realised this and as a result, more sustainable options are becoming available to us, thus making it easier for all of us to live globally-responsible lives.

When talking about global responsibility it is important to remember that money represents energy. When we choose to buy something, whether it is a toothbrush, a car or a cup of coffee, we are investing our energy in the company that produced the merchandise. We need to realise that with this investment comes a responsibility. By giving our energy to a company, we are supporting its ethical stance, as our energy will be used for furthering the operation of the business. The problem is that we are seldom aware of the ethical nature of the companies we support. If we were aware of many of the actions carried out with our energy, we would be sickened by our involvement. For instance, whenever we buy a fast food meal from a major fast food chain, we are almost certainly investing our energy in the deforestation of ancient forests and very often inhumane treatment of animals through bad farming practices. The globally conscious thing to do when choosing where to eat, would be to take into consideration the practices of the business or restaurant that we plan to support and to be sure to support the ones with the most environmentally and ethically-sound approach. Of course if we are in the middle of town and quickly need to grab something to eat we may not have time to start thinking about farming practices or ethical production. Certainly, if the awareness of wanting to choose the most globally conscious option is in the back of our minds, we will find that more often than not we end up supporting the better companies. We should not be afraid to follow our intuition as it is the soul's way of speaking to us in the midst of our busy lives.

General things worth bearing in mind when we do not have to make a split-second decision, include the manner in which the product is packaged, the chemicals of which it is comprised, where it was produced, how it was produced and by whom.

The wasteful usage of non-biodegradable plastics in the packaging of the products we buy is a major factor contributing to the pollution of our Earth. Whether it is in the form of an alarm clock, a soft drink bottle or a plastic packet, every scrap of plastic that we use has a polluting effect on our globe. It is important to avoid companies that use excessive amounts of plastic, and instead support companies that pursue other means of packaging in a more responsible fashion. The trouble with using this approach to choose which products to buy, is that sometimes the better products are packaged with more plastic than their poor quality counterparts. If we feel that we still want to support a business that uses excessive amounts of plastic, contact the company about re-addressing their environmental approach. We can never know what options could become available as a result of our efforts.

When we were living in Taiwan we learned to adapt our lifestyle in a globally-responsible direction from a sixty-five year old Buddhist friend of ours. This man is probably the most environmentally aware person I have been privileged to meet. He does not drive a car or motorcycle like most of the population does. Instead he cycles, sometimes travelling great distances, to avoid creating the harmful gases synonymous with motor vehicles. Taiwan has one of the best re-cycling systems around, but unfortunately the Taiwanese use plastic and other non-biodegradable matter everywhere. Though they are very good at recycling, they create waste at every corner, with every product and every meal. Also, due to the fast pace of the culture, many of the people (ourselves included during our stay) eat the majority of their meals out, or in the form of take-aways. The trouble with this, as we discovered, was that every time we bought a take-away meal it invariably came in a disposable bowl (cardboard, plastic or polystyrene) with disposable chopsticks in a disposable packet. Eating at the restaurants was seldom any better as many places favoured disposable cutlery and crockery over the re-usable types, to the degree where even the tablecloths were often thrown away after the meal.

Our friend (and others of a like mindset) could not let himself be responsible for such waste. Instead he carried around a shoulder bag containing a stainless steel bowl, a cup or glass and his own non-disposable chopsticks. He would simply ask the restaurant or shop to put his food in these containers instead of the disposable kind, thus resolving the problem. We decided to follow suit and bought ourselves a set of non-disposable eating gear, thus alleviating that particular strain on our consciences.

Something I might add at this point is the degree of apprehension that I initially felt when requesting that my food be put in our containers. For some reason I felt embarrassed to be different, to take a different road. But with a little perseverance this passed and I was able to see how well everyone responded to our decision to minimise waste.

Never feel shy about raising awareness of environmental issues. The more people raise environmental topics, the more likely they are to be taken seriously. The more pressure we put on the marketplace to minimise the use of non-biodegradable plastic, the sooner we will see an Earth-friendly plastic take its place. Already there are businesses looking to plant fibres, the likes of hemp, to produce Earth-friendly plastics. The more pressure we as the customers apply, the sooner we will see biodegradable and sustainable plastics on the shelves.

Always remember that your voice in the marketplace is your spending power. Be sure to be heard where you are most needed. Remember that whenever you cannot avoid buying plastics, it is imperative that you do your best to re-use and recycle as efficiently as possible.

Another key to becoming a globally conscious shopper is to become aware of the chemicals that make up the products we buy. For generations, we have been blindly supporting companies that use chemicals that are harmful to both the Earth and ourselves. Our soaps and detergents are amongst the worst of these. Nowadays it is easier than ever to find responsibly produced, Earth-friendly products to replace these harmful chemicals in our homes.

Next time you are at the supermarket, make a point of checking through the aisles to find the Earth-friendly products. If you cannot find anything, speak to the shop manager about stocking them.

I buy most of my household products from my nearest health shop. Earth-friendly toothpastes, soaps, detergents, washing powders and products are available at any good health shop. These are the sorts of companies in which we should be investing our energy, not the groups which are poisoning our world.

As with anything, making these changes is a slow process of finding the products that suit you best. You do not have to rush into your home and throw everything out all at once, but it will always be worth your while to persevere and slowly change to a more globally-conscious lifestyle.

Most of us are aware of the harmful emissions created by our vehicles. As a result, I probably do not need to mention how important it is to minimise excessive usage of our cars. We need to realise that our personal emissions count, because of the burning of fossil fuels, goes well beyond the running of our automobiles. For many, the electricity that powers our homes is derived from fossil fuels. Every light bulb that burns is responsible for the emission of carbon into our atmosphere. We would all do well, regardless of where our power comes from, to try and minimise wastage of electricity wherever possible. But our personal emissions count is only just getting started. What many of us do not realise is that every product we buy has its own emissions count and by buying it we absorb responsibility for the pollution. One of the major ways in which the things we buy require energy – and therefore create pollution – is the transportation of goods from their production site to where we buy and use them. The distance travelled by the products we buy is directly proportionate to the amount of pollution they create. The further goods travel the more fuel is required to move them and the more emissions they create. Hence the importance of buying locally produced products whenever possible. The globally conscious shopper needs to be aware of where his or her purchases have come from. This can normally be done by reading the label on the product a little more carefully, and never being afraid to ask.

Another benefit of buying locally is that it is easier to ensure the ethical maturity of companies close at hand than from those far away. The energy we invest through supporting businesses, makes us partly responsible for the way the employees of the company are treated. If we all began to take an interest in who is working behind the scenes of the companies in which we invest, then we would be able to stop the exploitation of the poor in sweatshops in third world countries all over the globe. The Internet provides us with the means through which to do this behind-the-scenes research and to see where we are pouring our energy. Websites such as www.responsibleshopper.com, compile information on the environmental and ethical nature of a lot of the big companies.

By taking the time to read up before we buy we can be sure that our energy is working in the right places. Of course, if we are still not sure which is the best company to support, it is always best to let our intuition guide us while intending to choose the best option.

The answer to returning our globe to a harmonious, healthy state lies in all of us becoming globally conscious. We need to become more conscious of our actions and the impact that they have on the Earth. We need to be sure to always choose the option that is most in line with living an environmentally friendly, ethically responsible, and sustainable lifestyle. The more of us who refuse to buy unethical, polluting products and instead support responsible, ethical, and Earth-friendly companies, the more companies we will see going in this direction.

Seth Falconer

Always keep in mind that All is One and that the intention behind all of your actions, no matter how big or small, affects everyone else. By living a globally conscious life, you are helping others change and in so doing, actively healing the Earth. Try your best not to become despondent with the situation no matter how hopeless it may seem. When you may not be able to see the answer to an environmental or ethical problem, remain positive and conscious, as by doing this you encourage those in the right positions to make the changes we need. Remember that we are all intimately connected to everything else and that your intention for change is fuelling that which you desire.

The time for humankind to transcend the illusion of separation from our beautiful planet has arrived. We cannot continue down our current path, killing our globe like parasites, feeding off her bountiful generosity and repaying it with slow and painful suffocation. We all need to become aware of, and take responsibility for our actions, to become globally conscious of who we are and what we are doing. Through doing this we can re-set the course of our lives to one that is in line with harmony and love, a paradigm where everyone and everything flourishes.

Turning Negativity into Positivity

As infuriating as it can sometimes be to hear, the old saying, 'If you have nothing nice to say, don't say anything at all,' is good advice to all of us. Neil Donald Walsch's series of books, Conversations with God[5], explains the reason for this very well. Within this series God clearly describes creation from the mind as a three-step process. The first of these three steps is, as always, thought. The second is word, both spoken and written, and the third is action. For the time being I would like to focus on his second step, word.

A lot of the thinking and thought processing that we do occurs entirely on a sub-conscious level. The acts of speaking and writing are synonymous with conscious thought. In order to speak or write about something we need to be conscious of our thoughts about it. As we touched upon in Part One, conscious thought holds within it far more creative potential than sub-conscious thought. Consequently, when we transfer our thinking into written or spoken words, we empower our thoughts and charge them with more creative energy.

With this in mind, it is easy to see that when we complain, we give more creative energy to that which we do not like. When we verbalise or write out disagreeable thoughts, we are effectively fuelling the further creation of experiences that we do not desire to repeat. Additionally, when we write down or say positive affirmations, we fuel them with creative energy. As a result, we need to become aware of the thoughts that we empower with words, and learn to distinguish between those that will serve our desires and those that will not.

It is important to know what we do and do not like. Naturally it is important to give thought, and sometimes words, to that which we dislike, but we need to be aware of where the divide lies between mentally exploring our opinions, and focusing on what we do not want to experience. It is necessary to think of and talk about contentious topics, but it is never necessary to complain about what our explorations uncover. Instead, we should focus our thoughts, along with our words, upon what we would like to see in the place of that which displeases us. When we shift from focusing on what we do not like, and instead, focus on what we would like to see in its place, the solution to the problem that lies before us is born. By choosing to pour our creative energy into a picture of the world that we like, rather than the one we detest, we are effectively creating the opportunity for change. Even though we may not be in the situation to embody the third step of creation – action, by thinking and talking about a new, more positive picture of the world, we empower those in the position to take the actions that will lead to these changes becoming a reality. In other words, choosing to focus on, talk and write about what we would like to see in place of a political situation that displeases us, brings the solution, be it a change in power, new legislation or a shift in the politicians' thinking, closer to becoming a reality.

Should we refrain from angry, sour and hurtful words and in their place utter words synonymous with what we desire, then we would break away from what we do not want and instead start creating our most wonderful picture of the world. When we do this, we will really begin to understand the splendour of our creative nature.

The main difficulty that we seem to have when trying to eliminate complaint from our lives, is that we do not know how to redirect our passion from that which angers or saddens us, to that which makes us happy. When we do not like something, our emotional tranquillity is disrupted. Much like a still pond that has a pebble dropped into it, negative stimuli sends ripples of annoyance, sadness or anger through our emotional waters, and so we often turn to blame and complaint as tools through which we seek to restore our emotional balance. Certainly, this strategy is fraught with the likelihood of creating further experiences about which to complain, so the need arises to create another more positively geared system to take its place. What we need to train ourselves to do is to identify that which we do not like, and, instead of focusing upon it, focus upon that which we would like to see in its place. Through doing this, we declare our intention to change the situation and as a result we open ourselves up to see the possible solutions to the problem before us. Another thing to remember when dealing with things that invoke negative emotions, is that everyone – each of us – is doing what we think is best. Let's face it, everything about the world that we perceive as bad is only so because of human actions. No one can call the growing of a tree in the middle of a jungle 'bad' or condemn the rain for falling. These things may seem bad should the tree one day fall on us or the rainwater flood our home but this is only so because of human action and, inevitably, of our own creation. These things are, of themselves, totally neutral. What really bothers us about the world is what other people do. I find it helpful to remember that even though others sometimes seem delusional and illogical or confused and cannot see things for what they truly are, they are invariably still trying to do what they think is best. Their approach may be flawed but they too are just people trying to make sense of a confusing world. This realisation places us in a position from which to transform the anger they invoke within us into compassion for a lost and confused soul. Thus we can turn away from creating more situations about which to feel angry and instead create healing feelings of compassion.

    At first glance, problems often seem impossibly unsolvable, but this is generally just because we are looking at the situation from a negative perspective. When we shift our focus onto the situation we would like to see in place of the problem, the 'impossible' will soon become a mere obstacle. Mother Theresa summed this point up beautifully in one of her more famous quotes. When asked why she had turned down an invitation to an anti-war rally, she replied 'People ask why I don't join the anti-war movement, and I say, I will join when you can show me a pro-peace movement.' She knew full well the futility of protesting against war and that pouring our energy into not wanting something is just the same as pouring our energy into wanting it. The I don't want's are just the same as the I do want's, so we must make sure the object upon which we are focusing is the end result of what we want to see, and not the current dislike that is before us.

While the movement from being anti-what you do not like, to being pro-what you do, is something that is directly applicable to our individual lives, it also applies to the attitudes of groups of all creeds and sizes. For instance, look at America's recent war against terror. In this instance, the governing body of the most powerful nation on Earth directly focused upon that which it did not want, and because of this, millions of people have been pouring their creative energy into bringing about more fear and terror.

These attitudes of aggression and brute force against what displeases us, have permeated our history. The time has come to address them. If we do not balance this futile, fear-driven mentality we have little hope of restoring peace and harmony to our world and we will almost certainly come to the sad end predicted by so many prophets of doom. If we do not learn to re-direct our creative energy, we are quite literally going to continue to create more and more to fight against, until we annihilate ourselves in the struggle.

The way to readdress this mis-focus of energy is to change the way we act when faced with something that upsets us. Instead of focusing on that which saddens or angers us, we should try to remember that all of us are trying to do what we think is best but not everyone has a strong spiritual foundation from which to work. We should try to feel compassion towards those who anger us and focus on what we would rather see in place of their actions. If we feel scared as a result of negative propaganda surrounding terrorism, we should focus on how safe and happy we are right now. When faced with sickness, we should focus on and be glad that we are alive; choosing to focus on life instead of death, health instead of sickness, will attract more life and health to us.

I remember house sitting for my parents' neighbours during winter some years ago. I was lying in a strange bed, wide-awake late at night, feeling really rotten. I had felt a cold coming on for a few days and it had finally arrived with a vengeance. Funnily enough, the worst symptom of this bout of the flu, or whatever it was, was a dull and persistent pain deep in one shoulder. I tossed and turned in bed, rubbing my shoulder and muttering to myself. At one point I decided that heat would probably help, so I ran myself a bath and, at two in the morning, soaked my shoulder. Nothing seemed to help. The hot water was appreciated by the rest of my cold body, but did nothing for my shoulder. Eventually I decided to try and meditate on the problem, to work out what this was all about. The answer was given that all I had been doing for many hours leading up to this point, was focusing my energy on the dull ache in my shoulder, exactly what I wanted to get rid of. Deciding that enough was enough I closed my eyes and focused on raising the vibration of my body to a level of great health. I focused on feeling and being healthy. Before I knew it I was fast asleep. When I woke up in the morning I felt fantastic. There were no signs of the cold, sore shoulder or lack of sleep at all. All that was required was for me to focus on feeling great.

....

Next time you feel ill, focus on health instead of sickness. If you think you are broke, look again at what you do have. Be grateful for the things you have and through this attitude of gratitude you will manifest more for which to be grateful.

Through this re-direction of creative energy you will begin to bring more of what you want into your daily experiences, replacing that which you no longer choose to know. In this way you can, by leading your life as a positive example, begin to instigate changes that will influence the larger governing forces of our societies.

....

All is One

An important tool for those of us looking to change our reactions from a negative to a positive format, is to become aware of what we allow to influence us. A lot of the changes we need to make to bring about peace, love and harmony, necessitate breaking away from the cultural reaction process offered to us by our modern consumer society. At present, our global society is more concerned with sucking all it possibly can from the present moment and greedily storing it away for the future, rather than enjoying it for what it is and cherishing it now. This poses a difficulty for those of us leading 'ordinary' lives, as to make the changes we feel need to be made, we need to go against conventional society, while immersed in it. It is important to ensure that we surround ourselves with the best possible influences to support the changes we want to see taking place.

Thankfully for those of us looking to be the change we desire, though our society may at a glance seem somewhat hopeless, our global culture is an extremely diverse entity. Because of this diversity, there is always a spot somewhere within the system that will give us the support and favourable influence we need to live our most beautiful picture of life. By this I do not necessarily mean relocating to a monastery in Tibet, where those seeking peace and enlightenment would surround us all of the time. We can make our supportive place exactly where we are right now through changing a few basic aspects of our surroundings and habits.

Firstly, it pays to become aware of what we are absorbing from the media, be it television, newspapers, radio or the Internet. Most of us try to ensure that we are reasonably well informed about the major current events. Sadly though, the majority of media facilities are preoccupied with bad news and, more often than not, tend to gloss over the miracles taking place all the time. This is a good example of having to work with a part of society we would like to see changed, while still needing to utilise what it offers. The negative, sensationalistic aspects of life upon which our media chooses to focus, are real and happening and in that sense it does pay us to know what is going on in our world. However, the benefit of this information is lost when we go beyond being informed and begin to support the negative views that we find before us. As always, there is a fine line to be drawn between being informed and being inundated to the point of furthering the atrocities about which we are informing ourselves. To balance the negative news, we should focus on the wonderful things happening around us all of the time. We never have to go far to find a display of love and happiness. It can be found in the feeling of green grass underfoot, a smile from a stranger, affection from a pet, the love of family or the embrace of a loved one. Whatever shape it takes, it is important to notice the good things happening all around us and not let the bad news consume our headspace.

We as humans are social beings. We thrive or wither as a result of the relationships we have with those around us. Because of this, it is of the utmost importance that we surround ourselves with people whose attitudes and actions support the best possible picture we have of the world. We should be around people who build us up to be the greatest we can be, not hold us back from achieving our full potential. How do our relationships serve us? We should be sure to change or eliminate those that do not further our most beautiful worldview, while taking care to grow those that do.

What we need to do to ensure that we begin to instigate the changes we wish to see is to ensure that our attitudes and reactions to negative stimuli are geared towards replacing the unpleasant reality with a better situation. Whenever we read, see or hear about something that we do not like, we should refrain from delving into the negative aspects of the situation and instead focus on what we would like to see in its place.

Although changing our individual contribution may sometimes seem to be a small portion of what our globe currently needs, we can take comfort in the notion that change accelerates in the same way that a snowball grows as it rolls down a snowy slope. With each turn, the snowball picks up more and more snow and the bigger it gets, the faster it grows. The movement for peace-orientated change is growing in this same way, except the snowball started rolling a very, very long time ago with the first recorded sages of our history, the likes of Jesus, Buddha, Krishna and Mohammed. That ball has been quietly rolling for a long time and is now at the point in its growth that, with each revolution, it grows by an immeasurably larger amount.

An example of this fast growing change is this book. Each person who reads this book or the many books like it, gains access to knowledge that was previously only available to very few people. If each person who reads this, changes her attitude towards what she does not like, and in doing so changes the attitude of another, who in turn changes the attitude of another and so on, the potential for change is immense, and the time that large-scale change would require is small.

Furthermore, we should remind ourselves that we not only influence others through the physical means with which we are so familiar. We are each a part of a divine energy that is expressing itself as human form. What we think and the intention behind our actions carries far beyond our physical form. Our thoughts and attitudes affect everything and everyone, because everything is connected. Everything is One. So when we make changes within ourselves for the greater good, our actions and intentions touch everyone else, whether they are aware of it or not. Even when we feel that we are not in a position to take physical measures towards re-balancing the problem before us, the positive thoughts we send out flow into the collective consciousness and are then able to be drawn upon by those in a situation to physically instigate the change we desire. We should always keep in mind our best possible picture for the world. The very act of thinking these thoughts is bringing that picture closer and closer to becoming a reality.

Our cosmos responds to a simple language, at the core of which lies the basic principle 'as you think, so shall it be'. Due to the close link between thought and words, this principle can be adapted to 'as you speak so shall it be'. The thoughts that we choose to empower with words are extremely powerful tools for creating what we want in the world, as long as we know how to use them. If we want to take responsibility for our lives and the role we play in our collective reality, it is imperative that we learn to focus our thoughts and words on feeling grateful for what we want — and not the wanting itself. If we do this, the cosmos will provide us with whatever we desire, for to do so it too is fulfilling its desires. Remember that everything is connected and that our desires are God's desires.

Belief, Intention and Expectation

Determine resolutely to expect only what you desire, then you attract only what you wish for.
Ralph Waldo Trine (1910)[6]

We can achieve what we believe, but we cannot achieve what we do not believe. As I state many times throughout this book, what we believe is what we experience to be true within our realities. It is often the case that to change the experiences we are having, we need to change our beliefs about how the world works. For many, this is difficult, as what they believe to be true is often the only way they have ever seen things to be.

....

If you are one of these people it would be wise to challenge your existing set of beliefs one small step at a time, each time choosing a change that you can stretch yourself to believe to be possible. The key here is to use the power of intention to bring forward the 'proof' you want to see. For instance, if you have been raised to believe that life is inherently difficult, but you feel you would like to change this perception, intend a stroke of good fortune to come your way. If you already are a fairly optimistic person, you may feel that it is possible for this good fortune to come about relatively easily, so intend it to happen within a short period of time, perhaps a morning. Or, if you are of a more pessimistic outlook, give yourself a day or even a week for the luck to find you, the point being to give yourself a time frame that you believe is possible. Then set about your life and see what happens. Be careful though, to expect this stroke of luck to come along within your designated time period. If you do not, and instead project doubt and negativity, you will counter the positive effects of your belief and intention. I guarantee that if you remain positive and really expect it, you will receive an unforeseen stroke of good fortune. If you do not, you either have not noticed what good things have come your way or you second-guessed yourself with doubt and disbelief.

All is One

When this first creative experiment has worked for you, take another slightly larger step and see what happens. Continue doing this and you will soon find that a new positive outlook will replace your old pessimistic beliefs about the world being a tough and nasty place. This technique is wonderful to change the experiences that make up your life and also to affect others on a global level. When you change your perception of any aspect of the world, you create an opportunity for others to do the same. Remember that your perception of life contributes to the creation of humankind's shared reality. When you contribute in a positive fashion, you raise the quality of life for everyone else as well as yourself.

....

It is through the merging of our three aspects of self that we become properly whole and begin to access the full potential of our creative ability. Not only this, but through the unification of the body, mind and spirit, our soul's divine understanding of the universe is able to guide us down the path we most need to travel in order to create the world of peace and love that we all deeply desire.

While we are human and do experience ourselves as individuals for a reason, the time has arrived for a global shift of consciousness towards a collective identity. We need to begin consciously using our intention, belief and expectation to purposefully create on a grander level. We each need to become aware of our creative nature on a global scale and ensure that what we are creating is the best picture we can possibly perceive. In order to do this, we all need to sit down and really think about what we would like to see out there in the world.

I, for one, would like to be living in a world where peace, happiness and harmony prevails. A world where everyone experiences love all the time and nobody goes without the basic needs of life. I would like to be living in a world of abundance and joy. So I do my best to keep this picture of the world in my mind's eye. I try to gear my creative nature towards this new view of the world through being grateful for the positive things in life and expecting more and more of them for us all.

Seth Falconer

If those who read this book join me in intending, believing in and expecting a world like this, perhaps we will all soon find ourselves living in a world where peace replaces war and violence. Where love replaces hate and is shared between us all, regardless of our small differences. Where joy is present in the hearts of every man, woman and child all of the time. A place where we all live in harmony with every aspect of our beautiful Earth, where we all realise and live by the notion that All is One.

....

A world of love, joy, laughter and harmony lies right around the corner waiting for us. All we have to do to make this world our reality is choose it, intend it and expect it.
....

References

[1] Emoto, Dr M. (2004). The Hidden Messages in Water. Oregon: Beyond Words Publishing.

[2] IMF. (2010). International Monetary Fund. Retrieved June 14, 2011, from http://www.imf.org/external/siteindex.htm

[3] CIA. (2009). Central Intelligence Agency. Retrieved June 14, 2011, from The World Factbook: https://www.cia.gov/library/the-world-factbook/geos/zi.html

[4] IUCN. (2011). The IUCN Red List of Threatened Species. Retrieved July 14, 2011, from: http://www.iucnredlist.org/

[5] Walsch, N. D. (1995). Conversations with God: An Uncommon Dialogue (vol. 1). London: Hodder & Stoughton.

[6] Trine, R. W. (1910). In Tune with the Infinite. New York: Dodge Publishing Company.

www.ingramcontent.com/pod-product-compliance
Lightning Source LLC
Chambersburg PA
CBHW022018290426
44109CB00015B/1227